Structured Workshops
The author presents workshops online and
in person in global locations for executives,
engineers, designers, technology professionals
and anyone interested in learning and applying
these proven innovation methods. For
information contact: info@curedale.com

50 Brainstorming Methods

For team and individual ideation

Robert Curedale

Dedication

Dedicated to aidan, liam, ashton and clayton

introduction

When faced with a difficult problem, one of the best ways of finding an effective solution is to organize a brainstorming session. Brainstorming is a group ideation method that was popularized by Alex Faickney Osborn in the 1953 book Applied Imagination. Brainstorming remains today one of the most powerful methods available for developing original ideas.

Brainstorming is a way of applying a collaborative approach to innovation. It is possible through brainstorming to leverage the different perspectives of a group and build on ideas put forward by others. In a brainstorming session, every person and every idea is of equal value. The wilder the ideas the better. It is important to have a comfortable safe environment where people feel that ideas can flow and that they will not be judged. It is important to generate many ideas quickly.

There are many different brainstorming methods. Different design practitioners can select different methods and apply them in different ways. You do not need to be an expert to participate in a brainstorm. The best results are obtained with a diverse team of participants which may include managers, designers, engineers, marketing, sales manufacturing professionals and end users of the product or service with people from different disciplines, cultures, gender, income and ages.

This book includes methods with a variety of different approaches to brainstorming. I have included a number of warming up exercises which will help your participants produce productive outcomes quickly. Western organizations are turning to innovation as a primary way of differentiating their offering.

The methods can be applied by designers and professionals working in design teams in all areas of design and architecture. These are tools to support a trend in most areas of design towards a methods based approach. The methods described have been tested and successfully applied across disciplines, across cultures, across the globe

I have kept the descriptions simple to give readers the essential information to adapt, combine and apply the methods in their own way. I hope that you will gradually build a personal toolkit of favored methods that you have tried and found effective. There is no best combination.

contents

Chapter 1
Thinking Approaches

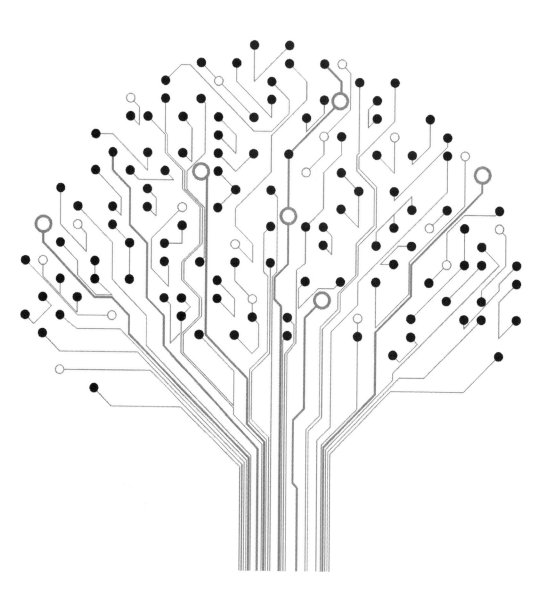

convergent thinking

WHAT IS IT?

Convergent thinking is a tool for problem solving in which the brain is applies a mechanized system or formula to some problem, where the solution is a number of steps from the problem. This kind of thinking is particularly appropriate in science, engineering, mathematics and technology.

Convergent thinking is opposite from divergent thinking in which a person generates many unique, creative responses to a single question or problem. Divergent thinking is followed by convergent thinking, in which a designer assesses, judges, and strengthens those options. Divergent thinking is what we do when we don't know the answer, when we don't know the next step

WHO INVENTED IT?

Hudson 1967,
Joy Paul Guilford

WHY USE THIS METHOD?

1. Convergent thinking leads to a single best answer, leaving no room for ambiguity.
2. Focuses on recognizing the familiar, reapplying techniques, and accumulating stored information

CHALLENGES

1. Divergent and convergent thinking need to be used together to solve many problems.
2. Designers and business managers are working on many problems which require divergent thinking due to changing complex environments.
3. Traditional management and engineering education stresses convergent thinking.

WHEN TO USE THIS METHOD

1. Explore Concepts
2. Make Plans

HOW TO USE THIS METHOD

Some of the rules of convergent thinking are:

1. Follow a systematic approach, find the patterns affinities and structure in a group of ideas.,
2. Use methods to evaluate ideas, assess qualitative and quantitative measures of ideas,
3. Avoid quickly ruling out an area of consideration, take your time.
4. Do not expend too much time in looking for the optimal solution of an ill-structured multi-criteria problem,
5. Assess risks and have a contingency plan.

REFERENCES

1. Cropley, Arthur (2006). "In Praise of Convergent Thinking". Creativity Research Journal 18: 391—404.

divergent thinking

WHAT IS IT?

The design process is a series of divergent and convergent phases. During the divergent phase of design the designer creates a number of choices. The goal of this approach is to analyze alternative approaches to test for the most stable solution. Divergent thinking is what we do when we don't know the answer, when we don't know the next step. Divergent thinking is followed by convergent thinking, in which a designer assesses, judges, and strengthens those options.

WHO INVENTED IT?

Hudson 1967,
Joy Paul Guilford

WHY USE THIS METHOD?

1. To an extent the number of choices created and compared during the divergent phases of design help determine the quality of the finished design.

CHALLENGES

1. Use when objectives are changing or ill defined.
1. Divergent and convergent thinking need to be used together to solve many problems.
2. Designers and business managers are working on many problems which require divergent thinking due to changing complex environments.

Image Copyright sippakorn, 2013
Used under license from Shutterstock.com

WHEN TO USE THIS METHOD

1. Frame insights
2. Explore Concepts
3. Make Plans

HOW TO USE THIS METHOD

Some of the rules for divergent thinking are:

1. Reframe the problem
2. See the problem from different perspectives,
3. Connect with and have empathy with the people that you are designing for.
4. Defer negative criticism.
5. Generate lots of ideas.
6. Combine and modify ideas,
7. Stretch the ideas, imagine ideas beyond normal limits,
8. Do not be afraid to break paradigms

RESOURCES

1. Pens
2. Paper
3. White board
4. Dry erase markers
5. Post it notes.

REFERENCES

1. Wade, Carole; Tavris, Carol (2008). Invitation to Psychology. Upper Saddle River, NJ: Pearson – Prentice Hall. pp. 258. ISBN 0-13-601609.

design thinking

WHAT IS IT?

Design Thinking is a methodology or approach to designing that should help you be more consistently innovative. It involves methods that enable empathy with people, it focuses on people. It is a collaborative methodology that involves iterative prototyping. It involves a series of divergent and convergent phases. It combines analytical and creative thinking approaches. It involves a toolkit of methods that can be applied to different styles of problems by different types of people. Anyone can use Design Thinking. It can be fun.

WHO INVENTED IT?

The origins of new design methods date back to before the 1950s. 1987 Peter Rowe, Professor at the Harvard Graduate School of Design, published "Design Thinking" the first significant usage of the term "Design Thinking" in literature. After 2000 the term became widely used.

CHALLENGES

1. There has been little research to validate claims about Design Thinking by advocates.
2. Some critics of Design Thinking suggest that it is a successful attempt to brand a set of existing concepts and frameworks with a appealing idea.

WHY USE DESIGN THINKING?

Design Thinking is useful when you have:
1. A poorly defined problem.
2. A lack of information.
3. A changing context or environment
4. It should result in consistently innovative solutions.

Design Thinking seeks a balance of design considerations including:
1. Business.
2. Empathy with people.
3. Application of technologies.
4. Environmental consideration.

Design Thinking seeks to balance two modes of thinking:
1. Analytical thinking
2. Creative Thinking

Advocates of Design Thinking believe that the approach results in consistently innovative design solutions oriented towards people.

Design Thinking takes a cross disciplinary team approach. It rejects the idea of a designer being a lone expert artist working in a studio remote from people in favor of an approach where a designer collaborates with a multidisciplinary team. Design Thinking advocates making informed decisions based on evidence gathered from the people and context in place of designers working on a hunch.

WHEN TO USE DESIGN THINKING

Design Thinking is an approach that can be applied throughout the design process:

1. Define intent
2. Know Context
3. Know User
4. Frame insights
5. Explore Concepts
6. Make Plans
7. Deliver Offering

RESOURCES

1. Paper
2. Pens
3. Camera
4. Notebook
5. Post-it-notes
6. Cardboard
7. White board
8. Dry-erase markers

REFERENCES

1. Martin, Roger L. The Opposable Mind: How Successful Leaders Win through Integrative Thinking. Boston, MA: Harvard Business School, 2007.
2. Buchanan, Richard, "Wicked Problems in Design Thinking," Design Issues, vol. 8, no. 2, Spring 1992
3. Cross, Nigel. "Designerly Ways of Knowing." Design Studies 3.4 (1982): 221-27.
4. Brown, Tim, and Katz, Barry. Change by Design: How Design Thinking Transforms Organizations and Inspires Innovation. New York: Harper Business, 2009.
5. Florida, Richard L. The Rise of the Creative Class: and How It is Transforming Work, Leisure, Community and Everyday Life. New York, NY: Basic, 2002 Basic, 2002
6. Jones, John Christopher. Design Methods. New York: John Wiley & Sons, 1970.

design thinking

FOCUS ON PEOPLE:

Design is more about people than it is about things. It is important to stand in those people's shoes, to see through their eyes, to uncover their stories, to share their worlds. Start each design by identifying a problem that real people are experiencing. Use the methods in this book selectively to gain empathy and understanding. and to inform your design. Good process is not a substitute for talented and skilled people on your design team.

GET PHYSICAL

Make simple physical prototypes of your ideas as early as possible. Constantly test your ideas with people. Do not worry about making prototypes beautiful until you are sure that you have a resolved final design. Use the prototypes to guide and improve your design. Do a lot of low cost prototypes to test how Your Ideas physically work. using cardboard, paper, markers, adhesive tape, photocopies, string and popsicle sticks. The idea is to test your idea, not to look like the final product. Expect to change it again. Limit your costs to ten or twenty dollars. Iterate, test and iterate. Do not make the prototype jewelry. It can stand in the way of finding the best design solution. In the minds of some a high fidelity prototype is a finished design solution rather than a tool for improving a design. You should make your idea physical as soon as possible. Be the first to get your hands dirty by making the idea real.

BE CURIOUS

Ask why? Explore and Experiment. Go outside your comfort zone. Do not assume that you know the answer. Look for inspiration in new ways and places. Christopher Columbus and Albert Einstein followed their curiosity to new places.

SEEK TEAM DIVERSITY

A diverse design team will produce more successful design than a team that lacks diversity. Innovation needs a collision of different ideas and approaches. Your team should have different genders, different ages, be from different cultures, different socioeconomic backgrounds and have different outlooks to be most successful. With diversity expect some conflict. Manage conflict productively and the best ideas will float to the surface. Have team members who have lived in different countries and cultures and with global awareness. Cross cultural life experience enables people to be more creative.

TAKE CONSIDERED RISKS

Taking considered risks is helps create differentiated design. Many designers and organizations do not have the flexibility or courage to create innovative, differentiated design solutions so they create products and services that are like existing products and services and must compete on price.
"It takes a lot of courage to release the familiar and seemingly secure, to embrace the new, but there is no real security in what is no longer meaningful. There is more security in the adventurous and exciting, for in movement there is life, and in change, there is power."
Alan Cohen

USE THE TOOLS

To understand the point of view of diverse peoples and cultures a designer needs to connect with those people and their context. The tools in this book are an effective way of seeing the world through the eyes of those people.

LEARN TO SEE AND HEAR

Reach out to understand people. Interpret what you see and hear. Read between the lines. Make new connections between the things you see and hear.

COMBINE ANALYTICAL AND CREATIVE THINKING

Effective collaboration is part of effective design. Designers work like members of an orchestra. We need to work with managers, engineers, salespeople and other professions. Human diversity and life experience contribute to better design solutions.

LOOK FOR BALANCE

Design Thinking seeks a balance of design factors including:

1. Business.
2. Empathy with people.
3. Application OF technology.
4. Environmental consideration.

TEAM COLLABORATION

Design today is a more complex activity than it was in the past. Business, technology, global cultural issues, environmental considerations, and human considerations all need careful consideration. Design Thinking recognizes the need for designers to be working as members of multidisciplinary multi skilled teams.

The need for creative self expression for designers is important. For an artist the need for creative self expression is a primary need. For a designer this need must be balanced by an awareness and response to the needs of others. Balanced design needs analytical as well as creative thinking. The methods in this book balance a designer's creative thinking with analytical thinking. This balance comes most effectively from a team rather than from an individual. Designers must respond to the needs of the design team, the needs of the business needs of those who employ us to design and the needs of those people that we design for.

design thinking process

DEFINE THE VISION?
What are we looking for?

1. Meet with key stakeholders to set vision
2. Assemble a diverse team
3. Develop intent and vision
4. Explore scenarios of user experience
5. Document user performance requirements
6. Define the group of people you are designing for. What is their gender, age, and income range. Where do they live. What is their culture?
7. Define your scope and constraints
8. Identify a need that you are addressing. Identify a problem that you are solving.
9. Identify opportunities
10. Meet stakeholders

KNOW THE PEOPLE AND CONTEXT
What else is out there?

1. Identify what you know and what you need to know.
2. Document a research plan
3. Benchmark competitive products
4. Create a budgeting and plan.
5. Create tasks and deliverables
6. Explore the context of use
7. Understand the risks
8. Observe and interview individuals, groups, experts.
9. Develop design strategy
10. Undertake qualitative, quantitative, primary and secondary research.
11. Talk to vendors

EXPLORE IDEAS
How is this for starters?

1. Brainstorm
2. Define the most promising ideas
3. Refine the ideas
4. Establish key differentiation of your ideas
5. Investigate existing intellectual property.

PROTOTYPE TEST AND ITERATE
How could we make it better?

1. Make your favored ideas physical.
2. Create low-fidelity prototypes from inexpensive available materials
3. Develop question guides
4. Develop test plan
5. Test prototypes with stakeholders
6. Get feedback from people.
7. Refine the prototypes
8. Test again
9. Build in the feedback
10. Refine again.
11. Continue iteration until design works.
12. Document the process.
13. When you are confident that your idea works make a prototype that looks and works like a production product.

DELIVER
Let's make it. Let's sell it.

1. Create your proposed production design
2. Test and evaluate
3. Review objectives
4. Manufacture your first samples
5. Review first production samples and refine.
6. Launch
7. Obtain user feedback
8. Conduct field studies
9. Define the vision for the next product or service.

critical thinking

WHAT IS IT?

Critical thinking is the discipline of rigorously and skillfully using information, experience, observation and reasoning to guide your decisions, actions and beliefs.

WHO INVENTED IT?

Socrates, Buddhist kalama sutta and Abhidharma.

WHY USE THIS METHOD?

1. More effective decisions
2. More efficient use of time
3. Rational rather than emotion-driven decisions.

WHEN TO USE THIS METHOD

1. Define intent
2. Know Context
3. Know User
4. Frame insights
5. Explore Concepts
6. Make Plans
7. Deliver Offering

HOW TO USE THIS METHOD

Critical thinking skills include:

1. Recognizing and solving problems.
2. Information gathering.
3. Interpreting information.
4. Recognizing relationships.
5. Drawing sound conclusions.
6. Leaning from experience
7. Recognizing assumptions.
8. Self criticism.
9. Self awareness.
10. Reflective thought.
11. Understanding meaning.

REFERENCES

1. Title: Critical Thinking Handbook: K-3rd Grades. A Guide for Remodelling Lesson Plans in Language Arts, Social Studies, and Science. Author: Richard W. Paul, A.J.A. Binker, Daniel Weil. Publisher: Foundation for Critical Thinking. ISBN: 0-944583-05-9
2. Paul, Richard; and Elder, Linda. The Miniature Guide to Critical Thinking Concepts and Tools. Dillon Beach: Foundation for Critical Thinking Press, 2008, p. 4. ISBN 978-0-944583-10-4
3. Ennis, R.H., "Critical Thinking Assessment" in Fasko, Critical Thinking and Reasoning: Current Research, Theory, and Practice (2003). ISBN 978-1-57273-460-9

critical thinking

"Critical thinking is independent thinking for oneself. Many of our beliefs are acquired at an early age, when we have a strong tendency to form beliefs for irrational reasons (because we want to believe, because we are praised or rewarded for believing). Critical thinkers use critical skills and insights to reveal and reject beliefs that are irrational.

In forming new beliefs, critical thinkers do not passively accept the beliefs of others; rather, they try to figure things out for themselves.

They are not limited by accepted ways of doing things. They evaluate both goals and how to achieve them. They do not accept as true, or reject as false, beliefs they do not understand. They are not easily manipulated."

Source: The critical thinking Handbook. Richard W. Paul

AFFECTIVE STRATEGIES

1. Thinking independently
2. Developing insight into egocentricity or sociocentricity
3. Exercising fair-mindedness
4. Exploring thoughts underlying feelings and feelings underlying thoughts
5. Developing intellectual humility and suspending judgment
6. Developing intellectual courage
7. Developing intellectual good faith or integrity
8. Developing intellectual perseverance
9. Developing confidence in reason

Source: The critical thinking Handbook. Richard W. Paul

COGNITIVE STRATEGIES
MACRO-ABILITIES

1. Refining generalizations and avoiding oversimplifications
2. Comparing analogous situations: transferring insights to new contexts
3. Developing one's perspective: creating or exploring beliefs, arguments, or theories
4. Clarifying issues, conclusions, or beliefs
5. Clarifying and analyzing the meanings of words or phrases
6. Developing criteria for evaluation: clarifying values and standards
7. Evaluating the credibility of sources of information
8. Questioning deeply: raising and pursuing root or significant questions
9. Analyzing or evaluating arguments, interpretations, beliefs, or theories
10. Generating or assessing solutions
11. Analyzing or evaluating actions or policies
12. Reading critically: clarifying or critiquing texts
13. Listening critically: the art of silent dialogue
14. Making interdisciplinary connections
15. Practicing Socratic discussion: clarifying and questioning beliefs, theories, or perspectives
16. Reasoning dialogically: comparing perspectives, interpretations, or theories
17. Reasoning dialectically: evaluating perspectives, interpretations, or theories

Source: The critical thinking Handbook. Richard W. Paul

COGNITIVE STRATEGIES
MICRO-ABILITIES

1. Comparing and contrasting ideals with actual practice
2. Thinking precisely about thinking: using critical vocabulary
3. Noting significant similarities and differences
4. Examining or evaluating assumptions
5. Distinguishing relevant from irrelevant facts
6. Making plausible inferences, predictions, or interpretations
7. Giving reasons and evaluating evidence and alleged facts
8. Recognizing contradictions
9. Exploring implications and consequences

Source: The critical thinking Handbook. Richard W. Paul

teaching critical thinking

STRATEGIES

1. Urge students to be reflective
2. Ask such questions as "How do you know", and "Is that a good source of information?"
3. Explore conclusions, explanations, sources of evidence, points of view
4. Discuss problems in the context of realistic situations that students see as significant
5. Ask "Why?"
6. Emphasize seeing things from others' points of view
7. Students do not need to become subject-matter experts before they can start to learn to think critically in a subject
8. Ask students to address questions to which you do not know the answer, or that are controversial. The question should seem significant to them and be interesting
9. Have them work on issues or questions in groups, with each group reporting to the entire class, and each person showing the others what he or she has done.

Source: Robert H. Ennis and Sean F. Ennis.

FRISCO

When appraising a position, whether yours or another's, attend at least to these elements:

1. F for Focus: Identify or be clear about the main point, that is, the conclusion
2. R for Reasons: Identify and evaluate the reasons
3. I for Inference: Consider whether the reasons establish the conclusion, given the alternatives
4. S for Situation: Pay attention to the situation
5. C for Clarity: Make sure that the meanings are clear
6. O for Overview: Review your entire appraisal as a unit

ABILITIES
Critical thinkers:
Care that their beliefs be true and that their decisions be justified;

- ◦ Seek alternative hypotheses, explanations, conclusions, plans, sources, etc.; and be open to them
- ◦ Consider seriously other points of view than their own
- ◦ Try to be well informed
- ◦ Endorse a position to the extent that, but only to the extent that, it is justified by the information that is available
- ◦ Use their critical thinking abilities

Care to understand and present a position honestly and clearly, theirs as well as others'; including to

- ◦ Discover and listen to others' view and reasons
- ◦ Be clear about the intended meaning of what is said, written, or otherwise communicated, seeking as much precision as the situation requires
- ◦ Determine, and maintain focus on, the conclusion or question
- ◦ Seek and offer reasons
- ◦ Take into account the total situation
- ◦ Be reflectively aware of their own basic beliefs

Care about every person. Caring critical thinkers

- ◦ Avoid intimidating or confusing others with their critical thinking prowess, taking into account others' feelings and level of understanding
- ◦ Are concerned about others' welfare

Source: Robert H. Ennis and Sean F. Ennis.

REFERENCES

1. Sobocan, Jan & Groarke, Leo   (Eds.), (2009), Critical thinking education and assessment: Can higher order thinking be tested? London, Ontario: Althouse Press.
2. Possin, Kevin (2008). A guide to critical thinking assessment.
3. CRITICAL THINKING Robert H. Ennis1996, Upper Saddle River, NJ: Prentice-Hall ISBN: 0-13-374711-5
4. HOW TO THINK LOGICALLY Gary Seay & Susana Nuccetelli 2008, 592 pgs. Pearson Higher Education ISBN 0321337778

critical thinking

"Critical thinking is independent thinking for oneself. Many of our beliefs are acquired at an early age, when we have a strong tendency to form beliefs for irrational reasons (because we want to believe, because we are praised or rewarded for believing). Critical thinkers use critical skills and insights to reveal and reject beliefs that are irrational.

In forming new beliefs, critical thinkers do not passively accept the beliefs of others; rather, they try to figure things out for themselves,

They are not limited by accepted ways of doing things. They evaluate both goals and how to achieve them. They do not accept as true, or reject as false, beliefs they do not understand. They are not easily manipulated."

Source: The critical thinking Handbook. Richard W. Paul

AFFECTIVE STRATEGIES
1. Thinking independently
2. Developing insight into egocentricity or sociocentricity
3. Exercising fair-mindedness
4. Exploring thoughts underlying feelings and feelings underlying thoughts
5. Developing intellectual humility and suspending judgment
6. Developing intellectual courage
7. Developing intellectual good faith or integrity
8. Developing intellectual perseverance
9. Developing confidence in reason

Source: The critical thinking Handbook. Richard W. Paul

COGNITIVE STRATEGIES MACRO-ABILITIES

1. Refining generalizations and avoiding oversimplifications
2. Comparing analogous situations: transferring insights to new contexts
3. Developing one's perspective: creating or exploring beliefs, arguments, or theories
4. Clarifying issues, conclusions, or beliefs
5. Clarifying and analyzing the meanings of words or phrases
6. Developing criteria for evaluation: clarifying values and standards
7. Evaluating the credibility of sources of information
8. Questioning deeply: raising and pursuing root or significant questions
9. Analyzing or evaluating arguments, interpretations, beliefs, or theories
10. Generating or assessing solutions
11. Analyzing or evaluating actions or policies
12. Reading critically: clarifying or critiquing texts
13. Listening critically: the art of silent dialogue
14. Making interdisciplinary connections
15. Practicing Socratic discussion: clarifying and questioning beliefs, theories, or perspectives
16. Reasoning dialogically: comparing perspectives, interpretations, or theories
17. Reasoning dialectically: evaluating perspectives, interpretations, or theories

Source: The critical thinking Handbook. Richard W. Paul

COGNITIVE STRATEGIES MICRO-ABILITIES

1. Comparing and contrasting ideals with actual practice
2. Thinking precisely about thinking: using critical vocabulary
3. Noting significant similarities and differences
4. Examining or evaluating assumptions
5. Distinguishing relevant from irrelevant facts
6. Making plausible inferences, predictions, or interpretations
7. Giving reasons and evaluating evidence and alleged facts
8. Recognizing contradictions
9. Exploring implications and consequences

Source: The critical thinking Handbook. Richard W. Paul

teaching critical thinking

STRATEGIES

1. Urge students to be reflective
2. Ask such questions as "How do you know", and "Is that a good source of information?"
3. Explore conclusions, explanations, sources of evidence, points of view
4. Discuss problems in the context of realistic situations that students see as significant
5. Ask "Why?"
6. Emphasize seeing things from others' points of view
7. Students do not need to become subject-matter experts before they can start to learn to think critically in a subject
8. Ask students to address questions to which you do not know the answer, or that are controversial. The question should seem significant to them and be interesting
9. Have them work on issues or questions in groups, with each group reporting to the entire class, and each person showing the others what he or she has done.

Source: Robert H. Ennis and Sean F. Ennis.

FRISCO

When appraising a position, whether yours or another's, attend at least to these elements:

1. F for Focus: Identify or be clear about the main point, that is, the conclusion
2. R for Reasons: Identify and evaluate the reasons
3. I for Inference: Consider whether the reasons establish the conclusion, given the alternatives
4. S for Situation: Pay attention to the situation
5. C for Clarity: Make sure that the meanings are clear
6. O for Overview: Review your entire appraisal as a unit

ABILITIES

Critical thinkers:

Care that their beliefs be true and that their decisions be justified;

- Seek alternative hypotheses, explanations, conclusions, plans, sources, etc.; and be open to them
- Consider seriously other points of view than their own
- Try to be well informed
- Endorse a position to the extent that, but only to the extent that, it is justified by the information that is available
- Use their critical thinking abilities

Care to understand and present a position honestly and clearly, theirs as well as others'; including to

- Discover and listen to others' view and reasons
- Be clear about the intended meaning of what is said, written, or otherwise communicated, seeking as much precision as the situation requires
- Determine, and maintain focus on, the conclusion or question
- Seek and offer reasons
- Take into account the total situation
- Be reflectively aware of their own basic beliefs

Care about every person. Caring critical thinkers

- Avoid intimidating or confusing others with their critical thinking prowess, taking into account others' feelings and level of understanding
- Are concerned about others' welfare

Source: Robert H. Ennis and Sean F. Ennis.

REFERENCES

1. Sobocan, Jan & Groarke, Leo   (Eds.), (2009), Critical thinking education and assessment: Can higher order thinking be tested? London, Ontario: Althouse Press.
2. Possin, Kevin (2008). A guide to critical thinking assessment.
3. CRITICAL THINKING Robert H. Ennis1996, Upper Saddle River, NJ: Prentice-Hall ISBN: 0-13-374711-5
4. HOW TO THINK LOGICALLY Gary Seay & Susana Nuccetelli 2008, 592 pgs. Pearson Higher Education ISBN 0321337778

Chapter 2
Warming up
get to know the team

team building exercises

WHAT IS IT?

An icebreaker is a short exercise at the beginning of a design project that helps the design team work productively together as quickly as possible. The duration of an icebreaker is usually less than 30 minutes.

They are an important component of collaborative or team based design. The Design Thinking approach recognizes the value of designers working productively as members of a diverse cross-disciplinary teams with managers, engineers, marketers and other professionals.

WHY USE THIS METHOD?

When a designer works with others in a new team it is important that the group works as quickly as possible in a creative constructive dialogue. An icebreaker is a way for team members to quickly start working effectively;y together. It is a worthwhile investment of half an hour at the beginning of a project and can be fun. Ice breakers help start people thinking creatively, exchanging ideas and help make a team work effectively. For meetings in a business setting in which contribute.

WHEN USE THIS METHOD

1. When team members do not know each other
2. When team members come from different cultures
3. When team needs to bond quickly
4. When team needs to work to a common gaol quickly.
5. When the discussion is new or unfamiliar.
6. When the moderator needs to know the participants.

common ground

WHAT IS IT?

An ice-breaker is an exercise that is used at the beginning of a design project or workshop to help to stimulate constructive interaction. It helps everyone to engage in the dialogue and contribute effectively.

WHY USE THIS METHOD?

1. Helps create a comfortable and productive environment.
2. Helps people get to know each other.
3. Helps participants engage the group and tasks.
4. Helps participants contribute effectively.
5. Creates a sense of community.

CHALLENGES

1. Be aware of time constraints.
2. Should limit the time to 15 to 30 minutes
3. Make it simple
4. It should be fun
5. You should be creative
6. Be enthusiastic
7. If something isn't working move on.
8. Consider your audience
9. Keep in mind technology requirements such as a microphone or projector.
10. Chairs can be arranged in a circle to help participants read body language.
11. Select exercises appropriate for your group.

WHEN TO USE THIS METHOD

1. Define intent

HOW TO USE THIS METHOD

1. The moderator ask the group to divide into pairs of participants
2. Each participant should select a group member that they do not know if possible.
3. Each person should interview the other person that they are paired with and make a list of 5 to ten things that they have in common.
4. One person from each pair should then present the list to the larger group.

RESOURCES

1. White board
2. Dry erase markers
3. A comfortable space

REFERENCES

1. Fergueson, S., & Aimone, L. (2002). Making people feel valued. Communication: Journalism Education Today, 36(1), 5-11
2. Sisco, B. R. (1991). Setting the climate for effective teaching and learning. New Directions for Adult and Continuing Education, (50), 41-50.

desert island

WHAT IS IT?

An ice-breaker is an exercise that is used at the beginning of a design project or workshop to help to stimulate constructive interaction. It helps everyone to engage in the dialogue and contribute effectively,

WHY USE THIS METHOD?

1. Helps create a comfortable and productive environment.
2. Helps people get to know each other.
3. Helps participants engage the group and tasks.
4. Helps participants contribute effectively.
5. Creates a sense of community.

CHALLENGES

1. Be aware of time constraints. Should limit the time to 15 to 30 minutes
2. Make it simple
3. It should be fun
4. You should be creative
5. Consider your audience
6. Keep in mind technology requirements such as a microphone or projector.
7. Chairs can be arranged in a circle to help participants read body language.

WHEN TO USE THIS METHOD

1. Define intent
2. Explore Concepts

HOW TO USE THIS METHOD

1. Moderator introduces the warming up exercise.
2. Each person has 30 second to list all of the things that they should take. Each person should list at least 3 things.
3. Each person should defend why their 3 items should be one of the chosen items selected by their team.
4. Each team can vote for three items preferred by their team.
5. Each of the teams presents the 3 items that they have agreed upon to the larger group.

RESOURCES

1. A comfortable space.
2. A moderator

REFERENCES

1. Fergueson, S., & Aimone, L. (2002). Making people feel valued. Communication: Journalism Education Today, 36(1), 5-11
2. Sisco, B. R. (1991). Setting the climate for effective teaching and learning. New Directions for Adult and Continuing Education, (50), 41-50.

expectations

WHAT IS IT?

An ice-breaker is an exercise that is used at the beginning of a design project or workshop to help to stimulate constructive interaction. It helps everyone to engage in the dialogue and contribute effectively,

WHY USE THIS METHOD?

1. Helps create a comfortable and productive environment.
2. Helps people get to know each other.
3. Helps participants engage the group and tasks.
4. Helps participants contribute effectively.
5. Creates a sense of community.

CHALLENGES

1. Be aware of time constraints. Should limit the time to 15 to 30 minutes
2. Make it simple
3. It should be fun
4. You should be creative
5. Be enthusiastic
6. If something isn't working move on.
7. Consider your audience
8. Keep in mind technology requirements such as a microphone or projector.
9. Chairs can be arranged in a circle to help participants read body language.
10. Select exercises appropriate for your group.

WHEN TO USE THIS METHOD

1. Define intent

HOW TO USE THIS METHOD

1. Each team member introduces themselves
2. Each team member outlines what is their expectations of the project.
3. Each team member shares their vision of the best possible outcome for the project.
4. Allow about 2 minutes per person

RESOURCES

1. White board
2. Dry erase markers
3. A comfortable space

REFERENCES

1. Fergueson, S., & Aimone, L. (2002). Making people feel valued. Communication: Journalism Education Today, 36(1), 5-11
2. Sisco, B. R. (1991). Setting the climate for effective teaching and learning. New Directions for Adult and Continuing Education, (50), 41-50.

diversity

WHAT IS IT?

An ice-breaker is an exercise that is used at the beginning of a design project or workshop to help to stimulate constructive interaction. It helps everyone to engage in the dialogue and contribute effectively,

WHY USE THIS METHOD?

1. Helps create a comfortable and productive environment.
2. Helps people get to know each other.
3. Helps participants engage the group and tasks.
4. Helps participants contribute effectively.
5. Creates a sense of community.

CHALLENGES

1. Be aware of time constraints.
2. Should limit the time to 15 to 30 minutes
3. Make it simple
4. It should be fun
5. You should be creative
6. Be enthusiastic
7. If something isn't working move on.
8. Consider your audience
9. Keep in mind technology requirements such as a microphone or projector.
10. Chairs can be arranged in a circle to help participants read body language.
11. Select exercises appropriate for your group.

WHEN TO USE THIS METHOD

1. Define intent

HOW TO USE THIS METHOD

2. The moderator introduces the exercise.
3. Place a number of objects or cards on the floor that represent the relative positions of the continents on a map of the earth.
4. The moderator asks each person to move to the spot where they were born.
5. When the group is in position the moderator asks each person to tell the group one thing about the place they were born.
6. Allow one or two minutes per person.
7. When this is complete the moderator asks the group to move to the place where they have spent the most of their adult life and tell the group one thing about that place.

RESOURCES

1. White board
2. Dry erase markers
3. A large comfortable space

REFERENCES

1. Fergueson, S., & Aimone, L. (2002). Making people feel valued. Communication: Journalism Education Today, 36(1), 5-11
2. Sisco, B. R. (1991). Setting the climate for effective teaching and learning. New Directions for Adult and Continuing Education, (50), 41-50.

finish the sentence

WHAT IS IT?

An ice-breaker is an exercise that is used at the beginning of a design project or workshop to help to stimulate constructive interaction. It helps everyone to engage in the dialogue and contribute effectively,

WHY USE THIS METHOD?

1. Helps create a comfortable and productive environment.
2. Helps people get to know each other.
3. Helps participants engage the group and tasks.
4. Helps participants contribute effectively.
5. Creates a sense of community.

CHALLENGES

1. Be aware of time constraints. Should limit the time to 15 to 30 minutes
2. Make it simple
3. It should be fun
4. You should be creative
5. Consider your audience
6. Keep in mind technology requirements such as a microphone or projector.
7. Chairs can be arranged in a circle to help participants read body language.

WHEN TO USE THIS METHOD

1. Define intent
2. Explore Concepts

HOW TO USE THIS METHOD

1. Moderator introduces the warming up exercise.
2. The moderator writes a question on the board such as:

"I would give anything to."
"The best advice I ever had was."

3. Each participant then introduces themselves and answers the question.

RESOURCES

1. A comfortable space.
2. A moderator

REFERENCES

1. Fergueson, S., & Aimone, L. (2002). Making people feel valued. Communication: Journalism Education Today, 36(1), 5–11
2. Sisco, B. R. (1991). Setting the climate for effective teaching and learning. New Directions for Adult and Continuing Education, (50), 41–50.

hopes and hurdles

WHAT IS IT?

Hopes and hurdles is a brainstorm that identifies factors that may help or hinder the success of success of a project:

1. Business drivers and hurdles
2. User and employee drivers and hurdles
3. Technology drivers and hurdles
4. Environmental drivers and hurdles.
5. Vendors
6. Competitive benchmarking.

WHY USE THIS METHOD?

1. This method helps identify where resources should be focused for most return on investment.
2. Enables stakeholders to understand other stakeholders expectations.

CHALLENGES

1. It provides a tangible focus for discussion.
2. It draws out tacit knowledge from your team.
3. It helps build team consensus.
4. It drives insights
5. Don't get too detailed
6. Some information may be sensitive.

WHEN TO USE THIS METHOD

1. Define intent
2. Know Context
3. Know User
4. Frame insights

HOW TO USE THIS METHOD

1. Define the problem.
2. Find a moderator
3. Brainstorm hopes and hurdles
   - Which are our own advantages?
   - What are we able to do quite well?
   - What strategic resources can we rely upon?
   - What could we enhance?
   - What should we avoid to do?
   - What are we doing poorly?
4. Collect the ideas on a white board or wall with post-it-notes.
5. Organize the contributions into two lists.
6. Prioritize each element
7. Use the lists to create strategic options.

RESOURCES

1. White board
2. Marker pens
3. Post-it notes
4. Flip chart
5. Video Camera
6. Camera

the interview

WHAT IS IT?

An ice-breaker is an exercise that is used at the beginning of a design project or workshop to help to stimulate constructive interaction. It helps everyone to engage in the dialogue and contribute effectively,

WHY USE THIS METHOD?

1. Helps create a comfortable and productive environment.
2. Helps people get to know each other.
3. Helps participants engage the group and tasks.
4. Helps participants contribute effectively.
5. Creates a sense of community.

CHALLENGES

1. Be aware of time constraints. Should limit the time to 15 to 30 minutes
2. Make it simple
3. It should be fun
4. You should be creative
5. Consider your audience
6. Keep in mind technology requirements such as a microphone or projector.
7. Chairs can be arranged in a circle to help participants read body language.

WHEN TO USE THIS METHOD

1. Define intent
2. Explore Concepts

HOW TO USE THIS METHOD

1. Moderator introduces the warming up exercise.
2. The group is paired into groups of two people who do not know each other.
3. The paired groups spend five minutes interviewing each other.
4. The interviewer introduces the interviewee to the group.
5. 3 minutes per person.

RESOURCES

1. A comfortable space.
2. A moderator

REFERENCES

1. Fergueson, S., & Aimone, L. (2002). Making people feel valued. Communication: Journalism Education Today, 36(1), 5-11
2. Sisco, B. R. (1991). Setting the climate for effective teaching and learning. New Directions for Adult and Continuing Education, (50), 41-50.

looking back

WHAT IS IT?

An ice-breaker is an exercise that is used at the beginning of a design project or workshop to help to stimulate constructive interaction. It helps everyone to engage in the dialogue and contribute effectively,

WHY USE THIS METHOD?

1. Helps create a comfortable and productive environment.
2. Helps people get to know each other.
3. Helps participants engage the group and tasks.
4. Helps participants contribute effectively.
5. Creates a sense of community.

CHALLENGES

1. Be aware of time constraints.
2. Should limit the time to 15 to 30 minutes
3. Make it simple
4. It should be fun
5. You should be creative
6. Be enthusiastic
7. If something isn't working move on.
8. Consider your audience
9. Keep in mind technology requirements such as a microphone or projector.
10. Chairs can be arranged in a circle to help participants read body language.
11. Select exercises appropriate for your group.

WHEN TO USE THIS METHOD

1. Define intent

HOW TO USE THIS METHOD

1. Divide people into groups of 4 people.
2. The moderator asks the group to imagine that it is the last day of the project.
3. Ask each person to imagine what they got out of the project and what the project has achieved and to explain it to their group of 4.
4. Each group selects the most interesting story and a spokesperson for the group.
5. The group spokespeople present the most interesting story for their group to the larger group.

RESOURCES

1. White board
2. Dry erase markers
3. A comfortable space

REFERENCES

1. Fergueson, S., & Aimone, L. (2002). Making people feel valued. Communication: Journalism Education Today, 36(1), 5-11
2. Sisco, B. R. (1991). Setting the climate for effective teaching and learning. New Directions for Adult and Continuing Education, (50), 41-50.

jumpstart storytelling

WHAT IS IT?

An ice-breaker is an exercise that is used at the beginning of a design project or workshop to help to stimulate constructive interaction. It helps everyone to engage in the dialogue and contribute effectively,

WHY USE THIS METHOD?

1. Stories reveal what is happening.
2. Stories inspire us to take action.
3. Stories are remembered.
4. Stories share and imbed values.
5. Stories connect people.

WHO INVENTED IT?

Seth Kahan

WHEN TO USE THIS METHOD

1. Helps create a comfortable and productive environment.
2. Helps people get to know each other.
3. Helps participants engage the group and tasks.
4. Helps participants contribute effectively.
5. Creates a sense of community narrative in the first 5 minutes of the project.

RESOURCES

1. Paper
2. Pens
3. White board
4. Dry-erase markers
5. Post-it-notes.

CHALLENGES

1. Be aware of time constraints. Should limit the time to 15 to 30 minutes
2. Make it simple
3. It should be fun
4. You should be creative
5. Consider your audience
6. Keep in mind technology requirements such as a microphone or projector.

Chairs can be arranged in a circle to help participants read body language.

HOW TO USE THIS METHOD

1. Divide the participants into groups of 5
2. Ask everyone to provide a story that is related to the objective of the workshop.
3. Each person gets 90 seconds.
4. Ask the participants to remember the story that resonated the most with them;
5. Reform the groups of 5 with different people.
6. Ask everyone to retell their story.
7. Note how the story improves with each retelling.
8. 90 seconds per story.
9. Ask each participant to reassess which story resonates with them the most.
10. Ask everyone to remember the person who told the most powerful, relevant, engaging story.
11. When clusters appear invite the people the group favored to retell their story to the whole group.

milestones

WHAT IS IT?

An ice-breaker is an exercise that is used at the beginning of a design project or workshop to help to stimulate constructive interaction. It helps everyone to engage in the dialogue and contribute effectively,

WHO INVENTED IT?

Ava S, Butler 1996

WHY USE THIS METHOD?

1. Helps create a comfortable and productive environment.
2. Helps people get to know each other.
3. Helps participants engage the group and tasks.
4. Helps participants contribute effectively.
5. Creates a sense of community.

CHALLENGES

1. Be aware of time constraints.
2. Should limit the time to 15 to 30 minutes
3. Make it simple
4. It should be fun
5. You should be creative
6. Be enthusiastic
7. If something isn't working move on.
8. Consider your audience
9. Keep in mind technology requirements such as a microphone or projector.
10. Chairs can be arranged in a circle to help participants read body language.
11. Select exercises appropriate for your group.

WHEN TO USE THIS METHOD

1. Define intent

HOW TO USE THIS METHOD

1. The moderator creates a milestone chart on a white board
2. The moderator estimates the age of the oldest members of the group and on a horizontal line write years from the approximate birth year of the older members to the present at 5 year intervals.

1960 1965 1970 1975 .

3. Using post-it notes each participant adds three personal milestones to the chart. One milestone per post-it-note under the year that the milestone occurred.
4. During the break participants read the milestones.

RESOURCES

5. Whiteboard
6. Dry erase markers
7. Post-it-notes
8. A comfortable space

REFERENCES

1. Butler, Ava S. (1996) Teamthink Publisher: Mcgraw Hill ISBN 0070094330

names

WHAT IS IT?

An ice-breaker is an exercise that is used at the beginning of a design project or workshop to help to stimulate constructive interaction. It helps everyone to engage in the dialogue and contribute effectively.

WHY USE THIS METHOD?

1. Helps create a comfortable and productive environment.
2. Helps people get to know each other.
3. Helps participants engage the group and tasks.
4. Helps participants contribute effectively.
5. Creates a sense of community.

CHALLENGES

1. Be aware of time constraints.
2. Should limit the time to 15 to 30 minutes
3. Make it simple
4. It should be fun
5. You should be creative
6. Be enthusiastic
7. If something isn't working move on.
8. Consider your audience
9. Keep in mind technology requirements such as a microphone or projector.
10. Chairs can be arranged in a circle to help participants read body language.
11. Select exercises appropriate for your group.

WHEN TO USE THIS METHOD

1. Define intent

HOW TO USE THIS METHOD

1. Divide people into groups of 4 people.
2. Ask each person to tell their group the story of their first and second name.
3. Allow 3 minutes per person.
4. Each group selects the most interesting story and a spokesperson for the group.
5. The group spokespeople present the most interesting story for their group to the larger group.

RESOURCES

1. White board
2. Dry erase markers
3. A comfortable space

REFERENCES

1. Fergueson, S., & Aimone, L. (2002). Making people feel valued. Communication: Journalism Education Today, 36(1), 5-11
2. Sisco, B. R. (1991). Setting the climate for effective teaching and learning. New Directions for Adult and Continuing Education, (50), 41-50.

places

WHAT IS IT?

An ice-breaker is an exercise that is used at the beginning of a design project or workshop to help to stimulate constructive interaction. It helps everyone to engage in the dialogue and contribute effectively,

WHY USE THIS METHOD?

1. Helps create a comfortable and productive environment.
2. Helps people get to know each other.
3. Helps participants engage the group and tasks.
4. Helps participants contribute effectively.
5. Creates a sense of community.

CHALLENGES

1. Be aware of time constraints. Should limit the time to 15 to 30 minutes
2. Make it simple
3. It should be fun
4. You should be creative
5. Be enthusiastic
6. If something isn't working move on.
7. Consider your audience
8. Keep in mind technology requirements such as a microphone or projector.
9. Chairs can be arranged in a circle to help participants read body language.
10. Select exercises appropriate for your group.

WHEN TO USE THIS METHOD

1. Define intent

HOW TO USE THIS METHOD

1. Each team member introduces themselves
2. Ask each team members to give three clues to a place that they are from, have been to or want to go to.
3. Give the team a few minutes.
4. Each team member takes two minutes to describe the clues. Other members of the groip guess the location.
5. The member describing the location reveals the location and describes it

RESOURCES

1. White board
2. Dry erase markers
3. A comfortable space

REFERENCES

1. Fergueson, S., & Aimone, L. (2002). Making people feel valued. Communication: Journalism Education Today, 36(1), 5-11
2. Sisco, B. R. (1991). Setting the climate for effective teaching and learning. New Directions for Adult and Continuing Education, (50), 41-50.

show and tell

WHAT IS IT?

An ice-breaker is an exercise that is used at the beginning of a design project or workshop to help to stimulate constructive interaction. It helps everyone to engage in the dialogue and contribute effectively,

WHY USE THIS METHOD?

1. Helps create a comfortable and productive environment.
2. Helps people get to know each other.
3. Helps participants engage the group and tasks.
4. Helps participants contribute effectively.
5. Creates a sense of community.
6. Helps group to collaborate and work as a team.

CHALLENGES

1. Be aware of time constraints.
2. Limit the time to 15 to 30 minutes
3. Make it simple
4. It should be fun
5. You should be creative
6. Consider your audience
7. Keep in mind technology requirements such as a microphone or projector.
8. Chairs can be arranged in a circle to help participants read body language.

WHEN TO USE THIS METHOD

1. Define intent
2. Explore Concepts

HOW TO USE THIS METHOD

1. Moderator introduces the warming up exercise.
2. Each person introduces themselves.
3. Each person selects one or two items from their pocket, wallet, purse or bag and explains why it is important to them.
4. 3 minutes per person.

RESOURCES

1. A comfortable space.
2. A moderator

REFERENCES

1. Fergueson, S., & Aimone, L. (2002). Making people feel valued. Communication: Journalism Education Today, 36(1), 5-11
2. Sisco, B. R. (1991). Setting the climate for effective teaching and learning. New Directions for Adult and Continuing Education, (50), 41-50.

time machine

WHAT IS IT?

An ice-breaker is an exercise that is used at the beginning of a design project or workshop to help to stimulate constructive interaction. It helps everyone to engage in the dialogue and contribute effectively,

WHY USE THIS METHOD?

1. Helps create a comfortable and productive environment.
2. Helps people get to know each other.
3. Helps participants engage the group and tasks.
4. Helps participants contribute effectively.
5. Creates a sense of community.

CHALLENGES

1. Be aware of time constraints.
2. Should limit the time to 15 to 30 minutes
3. Make it simple
4. It should be fun
5. You should be creative
6. Be enthusiastic
7. If something isn't working move on.
8. Consider your audience
9. Keep in mind technology requirements such as a microphone or projector.
10. Chairs can be arranged in a circle to help participants read body language.
11. Select exercises appropriate for your group.

WHEN TO USE THIS METHOD

1. Define intent

HOW TO USE THIS METHOD

1. The moderator asks each participant to describe where and when they would go if they had a time machine that could travel into the future or the past and to anywhere in the world.

RESOURCES

1. White board
2. Dry erase markers
3. A large comfortable space

REFERENCES

1. Fergueson, S., & Aimone, L. (2002). Making people feel valued. Communication: Journalism Education Today, 36(1), 5–11
2. Sisco, B. R. (1991). Setting the climate for effective teaching and learning. New Directions for Adult and Continuing Education, (50), 41–50.

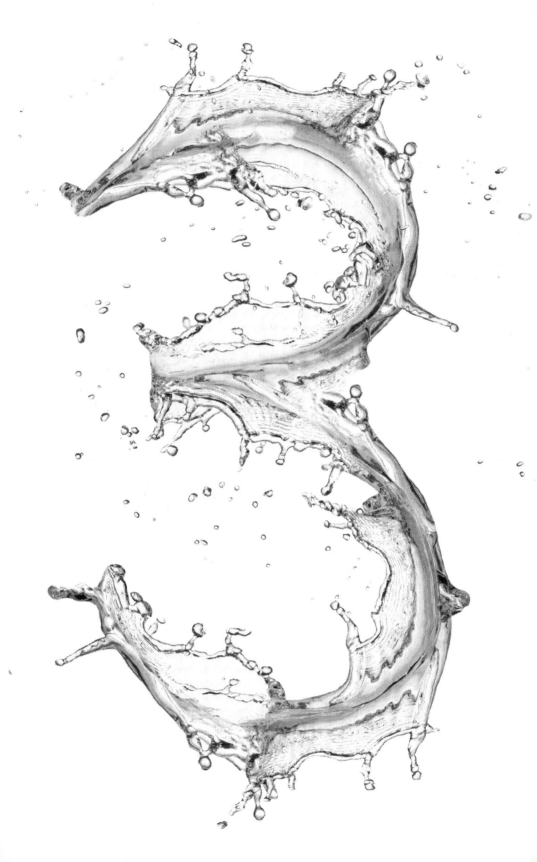

three in common

WHAT IS IT?

An ice-breaker is an exercise that is used at the beginning of a design project or workshop to help to stimulate constructive interaction. It helps everyone to engage in the dialogue and contribute effectively,

WHY USE THIS METHOD?

1. Helps create a comfortable and productive environment.
2. Helps people get to know each other.
3. Helps participants engage the group and tasks.
4. Helps participants contribute effectively.
5. Creates a sense of community.

CHALLENGES

1. Be aware of time constraints. Should limit the time to 15 to 30 minutes
2. Make it simple
3. It should be fun
4. You should be creative
5. Consider your audience
6. Keep in mind technology requirements such as a microphone or projector.
7. Chairs can be arranged in a circle to help participants read body language.

WHEN TO USE THIS METHOD

1. Define intent
2. Explore Concepts

HOW TO USE THIS METHOD

1. Moderator introduces the warming up exercise.
2. Break the larger group into groups of three participants.
3. Each group should find three things that they have in common.
4. After 15 minutes discussion each group should present to the larger group the three things that they have in common.

RESOURCES

1. A comfortable space.
2. A moderator

REFERENCES

1. Fergueson, S., & Aimone, L. (2002). Making people feel valued. Communication: Journalism Education Today, 36(1), 5-11
2. Sisco, B. R. (1991). Setting the climate for effective teaching and learning. New Directions for Adult and Continuing Education, (50), 41-50.

Chapter 3
Preparing for a Brainstorm

preparing for brainstorming

PREPARING FOR BRAINSTORMING
Come to the brainstorm session prepared.
1. Bring a lot of paper and markers.
2. Pens
3. Post-it-notes
4. Index cards
5. A flip chart
6. White board or wall
7. Video camera
8. Camera
9. One clear goal per brainstorming session.
10. Determine who will write things down and document the proceedings?
11. Allow one to two hours for a brainstorming session.
12. Recruit good people.
13. 8 to 12 people is a good number
14. Prepare a draft of initial brainstorm questions that you think will help guide the group.

CREATE A STRATEGY
1. What do you want to achieve?
2. What problem do you want solved?
3. Define the goal
4. How will you define the problem to the participants?
5. How long will the session be?
6. How many people will be involved?
7. What will be the mix of people?
8. Will there be a follow up session?
9. Will you send out information before the session?
10. Do the participants have the information that they need?
11. Who should you invite?
12. Assemble a diverse team.

13. Do the participants have the right skills and knowledge for the task?
14. Where will the brainstorm be held?
15. Who owns the intellectual property?
16. Will the session be free of interruptions?
17. How will you record the ideas?
18. What will you do with the information?
19. What brainstorming technique will be used and is it best for your purpose?
20. Be mindful of the scope brainstorm questions. Neither too broad nor too narrow.
21. 45-60 minutes for brainstorm time. Warm up 15-30 minutes.
22. Wrap up 15-30 minutes.

CHOOSING A TECHNIQUE
1. There are many different brainstorming methods.
2. Choose a method that suites your task and participants
3. Try different methods over time to find which ones work best for you.

REFRESHMENTS
1. An army marches on it's stomach
2. Offer tea, coffee water, soda.

SHOSHIN
1. Shoshin is a term from Zen Buddhism and Japanese martial arts. It means "beginner's mind". It refers to having an attitude of openness, eagerness, and lack of preconceptions even at an advanced level, like a child.

FACILITATING

1. Encourage everyone to contribute.
2. Review the rules and ask group to enforce them.
3. Put people in the right mindset and set tone with a quick warm up activity.
4. Encourage an attitude of shoshin.
5. Ask participants to turn phones off or onto vibrate mode.
6. A facilitator isn't a leader.
7. Do not steer the discussion
8. Don't let particular people dominate the conversation.
9. Keep the conversations on topic.
10. Set realistic time limits for each stage and be sure that you keep on time.
11. 5. Have a brainstorm plan and stick to it.
12. The facilitator should create an environment where it is safe to suggest wild ideas.
13. Provide clear directions at the beginning of the meeting.
14. Clearly define the problem to be discussed.
15. Write the problem on the whiteboard where everyone can see it.
16. Provide next steps at the end of the meeting.
17. Select final ideas by voting.
18. Use your camera or phone to take digital pictures of the idea output at the end of your meeting.
19. Good facilitation requires good listening skills
20. The facilitator should run the white board, writing down ideas as people come up with them,
21. Prevent people from interrupting others
22. Invite quieter people to contribute.
23. Hire a facilitator if necessary.
24. Start on time.
25. End on time.
26. keep things moving
27. You can filter the best ideas after the session or get the team to vote on their preferred ideas during the session.
28. Listen
29. Write fast & be visual
30. Use humour and be playful
31. Thank the group after the session.
32. Provide next steps to the group after the meeting.
33. Keep participants engaged
34. Encourage inter activity
35. 100 ideas per hour.
36. Avoid social hierarchy
37. Organize small break-out sessions that cut across traditional office boundaries to establish teams.
38. Encourage passion.

"Ways to affect the above and reframe the brainstorm on the fly:
- Pose a more specific question
- Rephrase a question
- Follow a thread that seems promising
- Shift gears and offer a whole new question
- Lob in a crazy idea
- Encourage people to move around, pace and play
- Say something funny"

Source Hasso Plattner Institute of Design Standford University

RULES FOR BRAINSTORMING

1. "**Defer judgment** Separating idea generation from idea selection strengthens both activities. For now, suspend critique. Know that you'll have plenty of time to evaluate the ideas after the brainstorm.
2. **Encourage wild ideas** Breakout ideas are right next to the absurd ones Build on the ideas of others listen and add to the flow if ideas. This will springboard your group to places no individual can get to on their own Go for volume best way to have a good idea is to have lots of ideas
3. **One conversation at a time** Maintain momentum as a group. Save the side conversations for later.
4. **Headline** Capture the essence quickly and move on. Don't stall the group by going into a long-winded idea. "
5. Focus on quanity not on quality.

POST-IT VOTING

1. Give every participant 4 stickers and have everyone put stickers next to their favorite ideas.
2. Each person tags 3 favorite ideas
3. Cluster favorite ideas
4. Clustering of stickers indicate possible strong design directions.

GROUP REVIEW

ask everyone to review the boards of ideas, a deas, and talk about the specific ideas or directions they like and why.

Source Hasso Plattner Institute of Design

THE ENVIRONMENT

1. Select a space not usually used by your team.
2. Refreshments
3. Find a comfortable quiet room
4. Comfortable chairs
5. No interruptions
6. Turn phones off
7. Go off-site. A new environment might spur creativity and innovation by providing new stimuli. Helps participants mentally distance themselves from ordinary perceptions and ways of thinking.
8. Location matters:
9. Make sure there are big visible materials for writing on
10. Keep the temperature comfortable Adequate lighting
11. Suitable external noise levels
12. A circular arrangement of seats is good where participants can read body language and with no "head of the table."
13. Seats should be not too far apart
14. Have a space with a lot of vertical writing space.

METHODS OF ARRANGING IDEAS

1. 2X2 matrix
2. Clustering
3. Continuums
4. Concentric circles
5. Timeljne
6. Pyramid
7. Prioritization
8. Adoption curve

group circle

WHAT IS IT?

This is a way of positioning your team members to facilitate open communication, brainstorming and ideas sharing. It is the best arrangement of people to enable reading of body language. Non verbal communication represents more than 80% of communication between people. It is an approach widely used in schools and in traditional societies for meetings.

WHO INVENTED IT?

Part of UK school teaching pedagogy.

WHY USE THIS METHOD?

1. Helps democratic communication.
2. Shifts responsibility from moderator top participants.

CHALLENGES

1. Communication is best without a table. A table may be necessary for some intended activities

WHEN TO USE THIS METHOD

2. Frame insights
3. Explore Concepts
4. Make Plans

HOW TO USE THIS METHOD

1. Between 5 and 20 people is the optimum number of participants.
2. Participants sit in a circle on chairs or around a circular table or on the floor on cushions.
3. Can pass around an object and when the person holds the object they can speak and the other participants listen

RESOURCES

1. Table
2. Chairs or cushions
3. White board
4. Dry erase markers
5. Paper
6. Pens

REFERENCES

1. Mosley, J. and Tew, M. (1999) Quality Circle Time in the Secondary School – A Handbook of Good Practice. David Fulton Publishers: London
2. Lloyd, G. and Munn, P. (eds) (1998) Sharing Good Practice: Prevention and Support for Pupils with Social, Emotional and Behavioral Difficulties. Moray House Publications: Edinburgh

incentives for brainstorming

Research suggests that incentives can augment creative processes. Participants were divided into three conditions.

1. A flat fee was paid to all participants.
2. Participants were awarded points for every unique idea of their own, and subjects were paid for the points that they earned.
3. Subjects were paid based on the impact that their idea had on the group; this was measured by counting the number of group ideas derived from the specific subject's ideas.

Condition III outperformed Condition II, and Condition II outperformed Condition I at a statistically significant level for most measures.

The results demonstrated that participants were willing to work far longer to achieve unique results in the expectation of compensation.

Source: Marketing Science Vol.25, No.5, September—October 2006, pp.411

Chapter 4

Brainstorming Methods

How do we create ideas?

brainstorming

WHAT IS IT?

Brainstorming is one of the oldest, fastest and most widely used creativity methods. Brainstorming does need to be undertaken by experts. It can be undertaken as a group or individually. Osborn believed that brainstorming as a group was most effective. Recent research has questioned this assumption. It should be used to address a single problem. Brainstorming is worthwhile when it is part of a larger process of design.

WHO INVENTED IT?

Alex Faickney Osborn 1953

WHY USE THIS METHOD?

1. It is useful for generating new types of solutions to problems.
2. Brainstorming allows each person in a group to better understand a problem.
3. It can be used to overcome creative blocks.
4. There is group buy-in to a design direction.

CHALLENGES

1. Groupthink
2. Not enough good ideas
3. Taking turns
4. Freeloading
5. Inhibition
6. Lack of critical thinking
7. A group that is too large competes for attention.

WHEN TO USE THIS METHOD

1. Explore Concepts

HOW TO USE THIS METHOD

1. A facilitator explains the problem to be explored and the process.
2. The problem can be written in a place where it can be seen by everyone participating
3. Defer judgment
4. Build on ideas to make them better.
5. Don't ridicule any idea.
6. One person speaking at a time.
7. Go for quantity the more ideas the better
8. No idea is too wild.
9. Stay focused on the problem
10. Be visual
11. Record everything.
12. Don't edit during a brainstorm
13. Preferred group size is from 2 to 12
14. A good facilitator should keep the ideas flowing.
15. Give a number of ideas to be generated for example 10 and time limit such as 30 minutes.
16. Analyze the results.

RESOURCES

1. Pens
2. Post-it-notes
3. A flip chart
4. White board or wall
5. Refreshments.

REFERENCES

1. Clark , Charles Hutchinson. The Dynamic New Way to Create Successful Ideas Publisher: Classic Business Bookshelf (November 23, 2010) ISBN-10: 1608425614 ISBN-13: 978-1608425617
2. Rawlinson J. Geoffrey Creative Thinking and Brainstorming. Jaico Publishing House (April 30, 2005) ISBN-10: 8172243480 ISBN-13: 978-8172243487

101 method

WHAT IS IT?

This is a brainstorming method focuses on creating volumes of ideas

WHY USE THIS METHOD?

1. Leverages the diverse experiences of a team.
2. A large volume of ideas helps overcome people's inhibitions to innovating.
3. Makes group problem solving fun.
4. Helps build team cohesion.
5. Everyone can participate.

CHALLENGES

1. Because the focus is on volume some ideas will not be useful.
2. Best used with other creativity methods

REFERENCES

1. Clark , Charles Hutchinson. The Dynamic New Way to Create Successful Ideas Publisher: Classic Business Bookshelf (November 23, 2010) ISBN-10: 1608425614 ISBN-13: 978-1608425617
2. Rawlinson J. Geoffrey Creative Thinking and Brainstorming. Jaico Publishing House (April 30, 2005) ISBN-10: 8172243480 ISBN-13: 978-8172243487

WHEN TO USE THIS METHOD

1. Generate concepts

HOW TO USE THIS METHOD

1. Define a problem
2. Select a moderator
3. Select a diverse design team of 4 to 12 people and a moderator.
4. The moderator asks the team to each generate 101 solutions to the design problem in a defined time. Allow 30 to 60 minutes.
5. Analyze results and prioritize.
6. Develop actionable ideas.

RESOURCES

1. Pens
2. Post-it-notes
3. A flip chart
4. White board or wall
5. Refreshments

method 635

WHAT IS IT?

Method 635 is a structured form of brain-storming. "

Here six participant gain a thorough under-standing of the task at hand and them sepa-rately writes three rough ideas for solution. These three ideas are then passed on the one of the other participants who read and add three additional ideas or modifications. This process continues until all participants have expanded or revised all original ideas. Six participants, three ideas, five rounds of supplements" (Löwgren and Stolterman 2004).

WHO INVENTED IT?

Professor Bernd Rohrbach 1968

WHY USE THIS METHOD?

1. Can generate a lot of ideas quickly
2. Participants can build on each others ideas
3. Ideas are recorded by the participants
4. Democratic method.
5. Ideas are contributed privately.

SEE ALSO

1. Brainwriting
2. Dot voting

WHEN TO USE THIS METHOD

1. Frame insights
2. Explore Concepts

Image Copyright Vitaly Korovin, 2013 Used under license from Shutterstock.com

HOW TO USE THIS METHOD

1. Your team should sit around a table.
2. Each team member is given a sheet of paper with the design objective written at the top.
3. Each team member is given three minutes to generate three ideas.
4. Your participants then pass the sheet of paper to the person sitting on their left.
5. Each participant must come up with three new ideas.
6. The process can stop when sheets come around the table.
7. Repeat until ideas are exhausted. No discussion at any stage.
8. No discussion.
9. Analyze ideas as a group,

RESOURCES

1. Paper
2. Pens
3. White board
4. Large table

REFERENCES

1. Rohrbach, Bernd: Creativity by rules – Method 635, a new technique for solving problems first published in the German sales magazine "Absatzwirtschaft", Volume 12, 1969. p73-75 and Volume 19, 1 October 1969.

alpha brainstorming

WHAT IS IT?

A brainstorming method that uses the alphabet for inspiration.

WHO INVENTED IT?

WHY USE THIS METHOD?

1. There is a hierarchy of ideas
2. This method generates many ideas.
3. This method highlights the connections between ideas which is the starting point for a design solution.

CHALLENGES

1. Groupthink
2. Not enough good ideas
3. Taking turns
4. Freeloading
5. Inhibition
6. Lack of critical thinking
7. A group that is too large competes for attention.

RESOURCES

1. Paper
2. Pens
3. White board
4. Dry-erase markers
5. Post-it-notes.

WHEN TO USE THIS METHOD

1. Explore Concepts

HOW TO USE THIS METHOD

1. The moderator introduces the method to the group.
2. The problem is defined by the moderator.
3. The larger group is broken down into groups of 4 or 5 participants.
4. One participant is asked to offer a solution to the design problem that starts with the letter A
5. The moderator records the ideas on a white board.
6. The person to the left of the first participant to present is asked to define a solution that starts with the letter B.
7. Continue until participants have proposed solutions starting with each letter of the alphabet.
8. The participants are asked to vote for their three preferred solutions.
9. Select the top ideas for further development.

aoki method

WHAT IS IT?
The Aoki or MBS method is a structured brainstorming method that stresses input by all team members.

WHO INVENTED IT?
Sadami Aoki. Used by Mitsubishi

WHY USE THIS METHOD?
1. There is a hierarchy of ideas
2. This method requires that a quantity of ideas is generated.
3. shifts you from reacting to a static snapshot of the problem and broadens your perspective toward the problem and the relationships and connections between its components

CHALLENGES
1. Groupthink
2. Not enough good ideas
3. Taking turns
4. Freeloading
5. Inhibition
6. Lack of critical thinking
7. A group that is too large competes for attention.

WHEN TO USE THIS METHOD
1. Explore Concepts

RESOURCES
1. Paper
2. Pens
3. White board
4. Dry-erase markers
5. Post-it-notes.

HOW TO USE THIS METHOD
6. Warm Up: Participants generate ideas for 15 minutes.
7. Participants present their ideas verbally to the larger group.
8. The larger group continues to generate ideas during the individual presentations.
9. For one hour the individual team members further explain their ideas to the group
10. Idea maps are created by the moderator.

REFERENCES
1. Clark , Charles Hutchinson. The Dynamic New Way to Create Successful Ideas Publisher: Classic Business Bookshelf (November 23, 2010) ISBN-10: 1608425614 ISBN-13: 978-1608425617
2. Rawlinson J. Geoffrey Creative Thinking and Brainstorming. Jaico Publishing House (April 30, 2005) ISBN-10: 8172243480 ISBN-13: 978-8172243487

analogies and metaphors

WHAT IS IT?
A method to help clarify an issue when exploring complex ideas. An analogy is a way of showing similarities between two different things. a metaphor is a representation of something.

WHO INVENTED IT?
Ava S, Butler 1996

WHY USE THIS METHOD?
1. Unstructured meetings waste time by trying to discuss all aspects of an issue at once.
2. This method saves time and improves the outcomes and efficiency of meetings.
3. Useful when discussing complex issues

RESOURCES
1. Paper
2. Pens
3. Whiteboard
4. Dry erase markers

WHEN TO USE THIS METHOD
1. Know Context
2. Know User
3. Frame insights
4. Explore Concepts

HOW TO USE THIS METHOD
1. Define the problem to be addressed.
2. The moderator introduces the problem and the method.
3. The moderator gives the group five minutes to consider appropriate analogies and metaphors.
4. Each participant presents their best analogies and metaphors to the group.
5. The group selects the best analogies and metaphors.
6. Summarize learnings.

REFERENCES
1. Butler, Ava S. (1996) Teamthink Publisher: Mcgraw Hill ISBN 0070094330
2. Clark , Charles Hutchinson. The Dynamic New Way to Create Successful Ideas Publisher: Classic Business Bookshelf (November 23, 2010) ISBN-10: 1608425614 ISBN-13: 978-1608425617
3. Rawlinson J. Geoffrey Creative Thinking and Brainstorming. Jaico Publishing House (April 30, 2005) ISBN-10: 8172243480 ISBN-13: 978-8172243487

backcasting

WHAT IS IT?
Backcasting is a method for planning the actions necessary to reach desired future goals. This method is often applied in a workshop format with stakeholders participating. The future scenarios are developed for periods of between 1 and 20 years in the future.

The participants first identify their goals and then work backwards to identify the necessary actions to reach those goals.

WHO INVENTED IT?
AT&T 1950s, Shel 1970s

WHY USE THIS METHOD?
1. It is inexpensive and fast
2. Backcasting is a tool for identifying, planning and reaching future goals.
3. Backcasting provides a strategy to reach future goals.

CHALLENGES
1. Need a good moderator
2. Needs good preparation

RESOURCES
1. Post-it-notes
2. White board
3. Pens
4. Dry-erase markers
5. Cameras

WHEN TO USE THIS METHOD
1. Define intent
2. Know Context
3. Know User
4. Frame insights
5. Explore Concepts
6. Make Plans
7. Deliver Offering

HOW TO USE THIS METHOD
A typical backcasting question is"How would you define success for yourself in 2015?
1. Define a framework
2. Analyze the present situation in relation to the framework
3. Prepare a vision and a number of desirable future scenarios.
4. Back-casting: Identify the steps to achieve this goal.
5. Further elaboration, detailing
6. Step by step strategies towards achieving the outcomes desired.
7. Ask do the strategies move us in the right direction? Are they flexible strategies?. Do the strategies represent a good return on investment?
8. Implementation, policy, organization embedding, follow-up

REFERENCES
1. Quist, J., & Vergragt, P. 2006. Past and future of backcasting: The shift to stakeholder participation and a proposal for a methodological framework. Futures Volume 38, Issue 9, November 2006, 1027-1045

banned

WHAT IS IT?

Banned is a method involving creating future scenarios based on imagining a world if a product, service system or experience did not exist and how people would possibly adapt.

WHO INVENTED IT?

Herman Kahn, Rand Corporation 1950, US

WHY USE THIS METHOD?

1. May uncover new design directions and possibilities not dependent on existing products services and systems.
2. Expose problems and opportunities.
3. Banned Scenarios become a focus for discussion related to a user experience. which helps evaluate and refine concepts. They can be used to challenge concepts through prototyping user interactions.

REFERENCES

1. "Scenarios," IDEO Method Cards. ISBN 0-9544132-1-0
2. Carroll, John M. Making Use: Scenario-based design of human-computer interactions. MIT Press, 2000.
3. Carroll J. M. Five Reasons for Scenario Based Design. Elsevier Science B. V. 2000.
4. Carroll, John M. Scenario-Based Design: Envisioning Work and Technology in System Development.

WHEN TO USE THIS METHOD

1. Know Context
2. Know User
3. Frame insights
4. Generate Concepts

HOW TO USE THIS METHOD

This exercise can be done individually or in group.

1. Decide the question to investigate.
2. Decide time and scope for the scenario process.
3. Identify stake holders.
4. Identify uncertainties.
5. Define the scenarios.
6. Can use with personas. Who is the persona? What is the experience? What is the outcome?
7. Create storyboards.
8. Analyze the scenarios through discussion.
9. Iterate as necessary.
10. Summarize insights

RESOURCES

1. Storyboard templates
2. Post-it-notes
3. Pens
4. Dry-erase markers
5. Video cameras
6. Empathy tools
7. Props

bodystorming

WHAT IS IT?

Bodystorming is method of prototyping experiences. It requires setting up an experience – complete with necessary artifacts and people – and physically "testing" it. A design team play out scenarios based on design concepts that they are developing. The method provides clues about the impact of the context on the user experience.

WHO INVENTED IT?

Buchenau, Fulton 2000

WHY USE THIS METHOD?

1. You are likely to find new possibilities and problems.
2. Generates empathy for users.
3. This method is an experiential design tool. Bodystorming helps design ideation by exploring context.
4. It is fast and inexpensive.
5. It is a form of physical prototyping
6. It is difficult to imagine misuse scenarios

CHALLENGES

1. Some team members may find acting a difficult task.

RESOURCES

1. Empathy tools
2. A large room
3. White board
4. Video camera

WHEN TO USE THIS METHOD

1. Know Context
2. Know User
3. Frame insights
4. Explore Concepts

HOW TO USE THIS METHOD

1. Select team.
2. Define the locations where a design will be used.
3. Go to those locations and observe how people interact. the artifacts in their environment.
4. Develop the prototypes and props that you need to explore an idea. Identify the people, personas and scenarios that may help you with insight into the design directions.,
5. Bodystorm the scenarios.
6. Record the scenarios with video and analyze them for insights.

REFERENCES

Understanding contexts by being there: case studies in bodystorming. Personal and Ubiquitous Computing, Vol. 7, No. 2. (July 2003), pp. 125–134, doi:10.1007/s00779-003-0238-7 by Antti Oulasvirta, Esko Kurvinen, Tomi Kankainen

boundary shifting

WHAT IS IT?

Boundary shifting involves identifying features or ideas outside the boundary of the system related to the defined problem and applying to them to the problem being addressed.

WHY USE THIS METHOD?

1. It is fast and inexpensive.

RESOURCES

1. Pen
2. Paper
3. White board
4. Dry-erase markers

WHEN TO USE THIS METHOD

1. Know Context
2. Know User
3. Frame insights

HOW TO USE THIS METHOD

1. Define the problem.
2. Research outside systems that may have related ideas or problems to the defined problem.
3. Identify ideas or solutions outside the problem system.
4. Apply the outside idea or solution to the problem being addressed.

REFERENCES

1. Walker, D. J., Dagger, B. K. J. and Roy, R. Creative Techniques in Product and Engineering Design. Woodhead Publishing Ltd 1991. ISBN 1 85573 025 1

brainwriting

WHAT IS IT?

Brainwriting is an alternative to brainstorming generating ideas by asking people to write down their ideas rather than presenting them verbally.

WHO INVENTED IT?

Brahm & Kleiner, 1996

WHY USE THIS METHOD?

1. Moderation of Brainwriting is easier than brainstorming.
2. Brainwriting tends to produce more ideas than brainstorming
3. Can be conducted in 15 to 30 minutes
4. Brainwriting is better if participants are shy or from cultures where group interaction is more guarded.
5. Brainwriting reduces the problems of groupthink.

CHALLENGES

1. Not enough good ideas
2. Freeloading
3. Inhibition
4. Lack of critical thinking

WHEN TO USE THIS METHOD

1. Explore Concepts

SEE ALSO

Explore Concepts

HOW TO USE THIS METHOD

1. Define the problem
2. Each participant should brainstorm three solutions in two minutes in written form.
3. Then have them pass the sheet of paper to their left.
4. Have the participants add to or build upon the existing suggestions by writing their own ideas underneath the original solutions. Allow 3 minutes.
5. The process should be repeated as many times as there are people around the table allowing an additional minute each time.
6. When you've finished post the ideas on a wall.
7. Get the group to vote on the most promising ideas.

RESOURCES

1. Pens
2. Post-it-notes
3. A flip chart
4. White board or wall
5. Refreshments.

REFERENCES

1. Clark , Charles Hutchinson. The Dynamic New Way to Create Successful Ideas Publisher: Classic Business Bookshelf (November 23, 2010) ISBN-10: 1608425614 ISBN-13: 978-1608425617
2. Rawlinson J. Geoffrey Creative Thinking and Brainstorming. Jaico Publishing House (April 30, 2005) ISBN-10: 8172243480 ISBN-13: 978-8172243487

benjamin franklin method

WHAT IS IT?
A method developed by Benjamin Franklin for making decisions.

WHO INVENTED IT?
Benjamin Franklin 1772

WHY USE THIS METHOD?
1. It is simple
2. It was developed and used by Benjamin Franklin who was a successful decision maker.

WHEN TO USE THIS METHOD
1. Explore Concepts

RESOURCES
1. Pen
2. Paper
3. White board
4. Dry erase markers
5. Post-it-notes

HOW TO USE THIS METHOD
Quote from a letter from Benjamin Franklin to Joseph Priestley London, September 19, 1772

"To get over this, my Way is, to divide half a Sheet of Paper by a Line into two Columns, writing over the one Pro, and over the other Con. Then during three or four Days Consideration I put down under the different Heads short Hints of the different Motives that at different Times occur to me for or against the Measure. When I have thus got them all together in one View, I endeavour to estimate their respective Weights; and where I find two, one on each side, that seem equal, I strike them both out: If I find a Reason pro equal to some two Reasons con, I strike out the three. If I judge some two Reasons con equal to some three Reasons pro, I strike out the five; and thus proceeding I find at length where the Ballance lies; and if after a Day or two of farther Consideration nothing new that is of Importance occurs on either side, I come to a Determination accordingly.

And tho' the Weight of Reasons cannot be taken with the Precision of Algebraic Quantities, yet when each is thus considered separately and comparatively, and the whole lies before me, I think I can judge better, and am less likely to take a rash Step; and in fact I have found great Advantage from this kind of Equation, in what may be called Moral or Prudential Algebra"

crowd sourcing

WHAT IS IT?

Crowd sourcing involves out sourcing a task to a dispersed group of people. It usually refers to tasks undertaken by an undefined public group rather than paid employees.

Types of crowd sourcing include:

1. Crowd funding
2. Crowd purchasing
3. Micro work

The incentives for crowd sourcing can include: immediate payoffs, delayed payoffs, and social motivation, skill variety, task identity, task autonomy, direct feedback from the job

WHO INVENTED IT?

Jeff Howe first used the term in a June 2006 Wired magazine article "The Rise of Crowd sourcing"

WHY USE THIS METHOD?

1. Crowd sourcing can obtain large numbers of alternative solutions.
2. It is relatively fast
3. Inexpensive.
4. Diverse solutions.
5. group of people is sometimes more intelligent than an individual

CHALLENGES

1. A faulty results caused by targeted, malicious work efforts
2. Ethical concerns
3. Difficulties in collaboration and team activity of crowd members.
4. Lack of monetary motivation

WHEN TO USE THIS METHOD

1. Define intent
2. Know Context
3. Know User
4. Frame insights
5. Explore Concepts
6. Make Plans
7. Deliver Offering

HOW TO USE THIS METHOD

1. Define your problem
2. Define your use of the crowd
3. Identify incentives.
4. Identify mechanism to reach the crowd.
5. Inspire your users to create
6. Distribute brief to the crowd
7. Analyze results.
8. Create preferred design solution.
9. Repeat above stages as necessary to refine the design.

RESOURCES

1. A social or other network
2. Crowd sourcing site or interface
3. A mechanism to reach the crowd.
4. An incentive for the crowd.
5. A crowd

REFERENCES

1. Howe, Jeff (2008), "Crowd sourcing: Why the Power of the Crowd is Driving the Future of Business", The International Achievement Institute.

dark horse prototype

WHAT IS IT?

A dark horse prototype is your most creative idea built as a fast prototype. The innovative approach serves as a focus for finding the optimum real solution to the design problem.

WHO INVENTED IT?

One of the methods taught at Stanford University.

WHY USE THIS METHOD?

1. This method is a way of breaking free of average solutions and exploring unknown territory
2. A way of challenging assumptions.

CHALLENGES

1. Fear of unexplored directions
2. Fear of change
1. Designers can become too attached to their prototypes and allow them to become jewelry that stands in the way of further refinement.
2. Client may believe that system is real.

WHEN TO USE THIS METHOD

1. Explore Concepts

HOW TO USE THIS METHOD

1. After initial brainstorming sessions select with your team the most challenging, interestingly or thought provoking idea.
2. Create a low resolution prototype of the selected idea.
3. With your team analyze and discuss the prototype.
4. Brainstorm ways of bringing back the dark horse concept into a realizable solution.

REFERENCES

1. Constantine, L. L., Windl, H., Noble, J., and Lockwood, L. A. D. "From Abstraction to Realization in User Interface Design: Abstract Prototypes Based on Canonical Components." Working Paper, The Convergence Colloquy, July 2000.

crawford slip method

WHAT IS IT?

The Crawford Slip method is a form of brainstorming that was developed in the 1920s and may have been the inspiration for most forms of brainstorming today. It was the origin of the method of brainstorming most common today. A moderator defines a problem statement, then participants record their ideas on 3 × 5 index cards.

WHO INVENTED IT?

The Crawford slip method was developed in the late 1920's by Dr. C. Crawford of the University of Southern California

WHY USE THIS METHOD?

1. Any size group
2. Commonly used for 50 to 200 participants but can be used for up to 5,000 people.
3. Any seating arrangement.
4. Broader participation (includes less expressive participants).
5. Large quantity of ideas.
6. Good for sensitive topics since participants' input is anonymous, without team interaction.
7. Easier process of sorting ideas.

CHALLENGES

1. May be a slow process.
2. Written ideas may need to be explained verbally.
3. Written ideas may be stated as a word if a detailed description would be too long.
4. All members participate.

WHEN TO USE THIS METHOD

1. Explore Concepts

HOW TO USE THIS METHOD

1. Define the problem
2. Distribute 3 inch by 5 inch blank index cards to each team member. 20 cards each may be a suitable number.
3. The moderator writes the problem statement on a white board.
4. Participants spend 20 minutes to 40 minutes generating ideas and describing one idea per index card with sketches or written descriptions. One sentence or idea per card.
5. The cards are returned to the moderator and spread out on a large table.
6. The cards are sorted into between 3 and 10 large categories. The categories depend on the problem and are generated by the team through discussion.
7. The categories are prioritized.

RESOURCES

1. Pens
2. Paper
3. 3 X 5 inch index cards

REFERENCES

1. Dettmer H, W. Brainpower Networking Using the Crawford Slip Method. Publisher: Trafford (October 2003) ISBN-10: 141200909X ISBN-13: 978-1412009096

digital method

WHAT IS IT?

This brainstorming method uses an electronic meeting system or e-mail.

WHY USE THIS METHOD?

1. Ideas are automatically recorded.
2. This method requires that a quantity of ideas is generated.
3. The session can be a short duration such as 30 minutes or over a long duration such as 2 weeks.
4. Enables much larger groups to brainstorm on a topic than would normally be productive in a traditional brainstorming session

CHALLENGES

1. Groupthink
2. Not enough good ideas
3. Taking turns
4. Freeloading
5. Inhibition
6. Lack of critical thinking

WHEN TO USE THIS METHOD

1. Explore Concepts

RESOURCES

1. Computer
2. Internet connection
3. Brainstorming software
4. E-mail
5. Electronic meeting system.

HOW TO USE THIS METHOD

1. Define a problem to be explored
2. Appoint a moderator.
3. Each participant connects through an electronic meeting system
4. Participants share ideas
5. Ideas are immediately visible to the group
6. Ideas are often anonymously posted or through avatars.
7. Review the contributions.

disney method

WHAT IS IT?

The Disney method is a parallel thinking technique. It allows a team to discuss an issue from four perspectives. It involves parallel thinking to analyze a problem, generate ideas, evaluate ideas, and to create a strategy. It is a method used in workshops. The four thinking perspectives are – Spectators, Dreamers, Realist's and Critics.

WHO INVENTED IT?

Dilts, 1991

WHY USE THIS METHOD?

1. Allows the group top discuss a problem from four different perspectives

CHALLENGES

1. An alternative to De Bono Six hat Method.
2. Will deliver a workable solution quickly.

WHEN TO USE THIS METHOD

1. Explore Concepts

HOW TO USE THIS METHOD

1. At the end of each of the four sessions the participants leave the room and then at a later time reenter the room then assuming the personas and perspectives of the next group. Time taken is often 60 to 90 minutes in total.
2. The spectator's view. Puts the problem in an external context. How would a consultant, a customer or an outside observer view the problem?

3. The Dreamers view. Looking for an ideal solution. What would our dream solution for this be? What if? Unconstrained brainstorm. Defer judgement. Divergent thinking. What do we desire? If we could have unlimited resources what would we do? They list their ideas on the white board.

4. Realists view. The realists are convergent thinkers. How can we turn the dreamer's views into reality? Looking for ideas that are feasible, profitable, customer focused and can be implemented within 18 months. They look through the dreamer's ideas on the white board and narrow them down to a short list, discuss them and choose the single best idea and create an implementation plan. What steps are necessary to implement this idea? Who can approve it, how much funding is needed? They draw the plan on the whiteboard and then leave the room.

5. The Critics view. What are the risks and obstacles? Who would oppose this plan? What could go wrong? Refine, improve or reject. Be constructive. This group defines the risks and obstacles, make some suggestions and write down these ideas on the white board.

RESOURCES

1. White board
2. Dry erase markers.
3. Pens
4. Post-it-notes.
5. A private room

five points

WHAT IS IT?

This method is a way of selecting a concept direction from a number of alternatives based on the preferences of your design team. Each participant is given five points to distribute between the concepts they like the most.

WHY USE THIS METHOD?

1. It is a fast and effective way of selecting the best concepts to develop.

CHALLENGES

1. Can be subjective
2. Team members can influence voting by the strength of their personality.

WHEN TO USE THIS METHOD

1. Explore Concepts

RESOURCES

1. Pen
2. Paper
3. White board
4. Dry erase markers

HOW TO USE THIS METHOD

1. Assemble your design team.
2. Brainstorm concepts
3. Pin the concepts on a wall
4. Team members present their ideas to the group.
5. Each team member is given five points to allocate to the concepts
6. This method works best if your team is between 4 and 12 people and a diverse cross disciplinary team
7. Each team member has five points to allocate.
8. They can allocate them all to one idea or distribute the points between several ideas.
9. Team members shouldn't vote for their own ideas.
10. Total the points and develop the ideas with most points in a further brainstorming session.

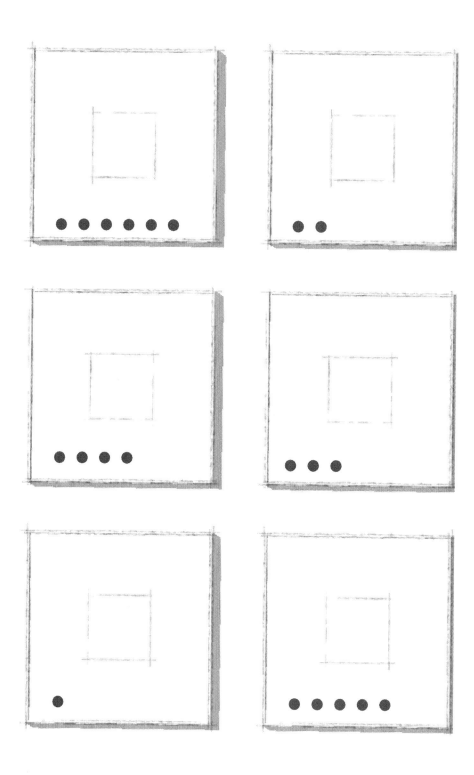

dot voting

WHAT IS IT?

This method is a collective way of prioritizing and converging on a design solution that uses group wisdom. Concepts can be individually scored against selection criteria such as the business proposition, ease of manufacturing, cost and usability. Each participant scores each concept against a list of assessment criteria and the scores are totaled to determine the favored ideas.

WHY USE THIS METHOD?

It is a method of selecting a favored idea by collective rather than individual judgment. It is a fast method that allows a design to progress. It leverages the strengths of diverse team member viewpoints and experiences.

CHALLENGES

1. The assessment is subjective.
2. Groupthink
3. Not enough good ideas
4. Inhibition
5. Lack of critical thinking

RESOURCES

1. Large wall
2. Adhesive dots

REFERENCES

1. Dotmocracy handbook Jason Diceman Version 2.2 March 2010 ISBN 45152708X EAN-13 9781451527087

WHEN TO USE THIS METHOD

1. Define intent
2. Know Context
3. Know User
4. Frame insights
5. Explore Concepts
6. Make Plans
7. Deliver Offering

HOW TO USE THIS METHOD

1. Select a team of between 4 and 20 cross disciplinary participants.
2. Brainstorm ideas for example ask each team member to generate six ideas as sketches.
3. Each idea should be presented on one post it note or page.
4. Each designer should quickly explain each idea to the group before the group votes.
5. Spread the ideas over a wall or table.
6. Ask the team to group the ideas by similarity or affinity.
7. Ask the team to vote on their two or three favorite ideas and total the votes. You can use sticky dots or colored pins to indicate a vote or a moderator can tally the scores.
8. Rearrange the ideas so that the ideas with the dots are grouped together, ranked from most dots to least.
9. Talk about the ideas that received the most votes and see if there is a general level of comfort with taking one or more of those ideas to the next step.

DOUBLE REVERSAL PROCESS

1

PREVIOUSLY BRAINSTORMED IDEAS

2

REVERSE THE PROBLEM
BRAINSTORM NEW IDEAS

3

REVERSE THE REVERSED
PROBLEM IDEAS

4

ADD NEW IDEAS TO PREVIOUSLY
BRAINSTORMED IDEAS

double reversal

WHAT IS IT?

The double reversal is a reversed thinking process that allows teams to continue with idea generating after they have run out of ideas or simply have found no novel way of looking at the problem. This tool requires an issue, idea, or goal to be reversed or stated in a negative form in order to gain more ideas of what could cause the problem. Reversing again each reversed idea should produce potential action steps to consider in the problem solution phase.

WHY USE THIS METHOD?

1. To identify new solutions for a design problem.
1. To expaand a list of previously brainstormed ideas.
1. To take a new perspective after an unproductive brainstorming effort.

WHEN TO USE THIS METHOD

1. Explore Concepts

HOW TO USE THIS METHOD

1. Start with a collection of previously brainstormed ideas.
2. Display the ideas and discuss them with your team.
3. Reverse the objective.
4. Your team brainstorms how to make the problem worse with each idea.
5. Record the ideas on a white boardthe double reversal process.
6. The team reverses the ideas. A double reversal.
7. Add the new set of ideas to the original set.

RESOURCES

1. Pens
2. Paper
3. White board
4. Dry erase markers
5. Post it notes.

dramaturgy

WHAT IS IT?
Dramaturgy is a method that uses drama techniques to help understand user behaviors and needs. It a form of prototyping.

WHO INVENTED IT?
Robert, Benford D., and Scott A. Hunt

WHY USE THIS METHOD?
1. Created to make personas more dynamic.

CHALLENGES
1. Some team members may be uncomfortable with drama based activity.
2. The method is not in context
3. The method may be subjective as it does not involve the people being designed for,

WHEN TO USE THIS METHOD
4. Know Context
5. Know User
6. Frame insights
7. Explore Concepts

HOW TO USE THIS METHOD
1. Choose a character
2. Create groups of 2 or 3 members of your design team
3. Ask your teams to write monologues for the characters based on public, private and intimate levels.
4. Ask your team to discuss the rituals of the character's lives
5. Ask your team to create maps of the stakeholders
6. Create scenes exploring crucial moments in your character's experiences or interactions.
7. Present these scenarios with groups of actors.
8. Explore the problems and challenges of the character's experiences and interactions.

REFERENCES
1. Robert, Benford D., and Scott A. Hunt. "Dramaturgy and Social Movements: The Social Construction and Communication of Power." Social Inquiry 62.1 (2007): 36-55. Wiley Online Library.

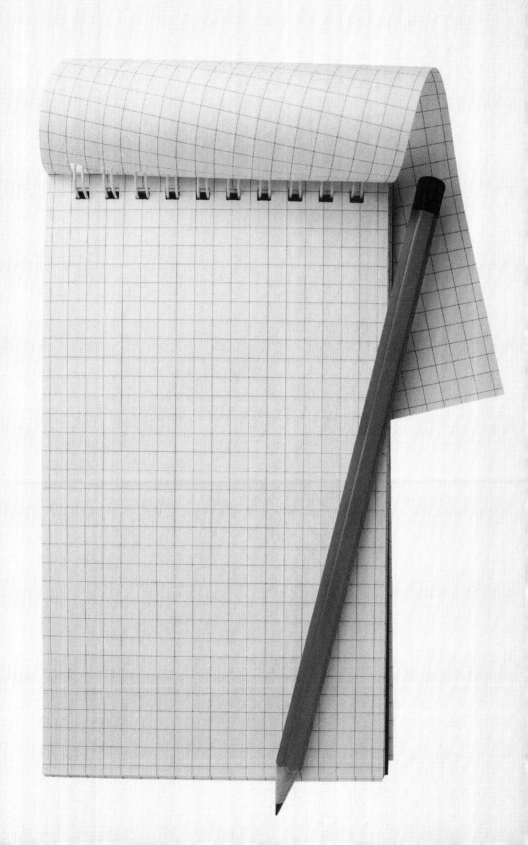

freewriting

WHAT IS IT?

WHO INVENTED IT?
Alex Faickney Osborn 1953 is often credited with inventing brainstorming.

WHY USE THIS METHOD?
1. There is a hierarchy of ideas
2. This method generates many ideas.
3. This method highlights the connections between ideas which is the starting point for a design solution.

CHALLENGES
1. Groupthink
2. Not enough good ideas
3. Taking turns
4. Freeloading
5. Inhibition
6. Lack of critical thinking
7. A group that is too large competes for attention.

RESOURCES
1. Paper
2. Pens
3. White board
4. Dry-erase markers
5. Post-it-notes.

WHEN TO USE THIS METHOD
1. Explore Concepts

HOW TO USE THIS METHOD
1. The moderator introduces the method to the group.
2. The problem is defined by the moderator.
3. The moderator instructs the participants to begin writing about the design problem and not to stop until the time is up.
4. Allow ten minutes and give each participant 10 to 20 pages of blank copy paper.
5. After ten minutes each participant passes the pages that they have written to the participant on their left.
6. Each participant reviews the written material, underlines ideas that they find interesting and is asked to provide a one sentence summary of the content
7. Allow ten minutes.
8. After ten minutes each participant presents their underlined ideas and summary to the group.
9. The group selects the most interesting ideas for further development.

go and no go

WHAT IS IT?
A method to determine when your team is ready to move on to the next discussion item in a meeting.

WHO INVENTED IT?
Ava S, Butler 1996

WHY USE THIS METHOD?
1. Unstructured meetings waste time by trying to discuss all aspects of an issue at once.
2. This method saves time and improves the outcomes and efficiency of meetings.
3. Useful when discussing complex issues

RESOURCES
1. Paper
2. Pens
3. Whiteboard
4. Dry erase markers

WHEN TO USE THIS METHOD
1. Define intent
2. Make Plans

HOW TO USE THIS METHOD
1. When the moderator thinks that it is time to move on to the next agenda item ask:
   ◦ "All in favor of moving on to the next agenda item say Go"
   ◦ "All in favor of not moving forward say No Go"
2. If there are more no go votes the moderator asks "what needs to happen before we will feel comfortable moving forward?"
3. Iterate if necessary.

REFERENCES
1. Butler, Ava S. (1996) Teamthink Publisher: Mcgraw Hill ISBN 0070094330

When dreams come true
BELIEVE IT

greeting cards

WHAT IS IT?
This is a group creativity method that uses greeting cards as a focus to stimulate ideas.

WHO INVENTED IT?
James Pickens 1981

WHY USE THIS METHOD?
1. It is a way to build team collaboration and stimulate ideas.

RESOURCES
2. Paste
3. Scissors
4. Magazines
5. Thick A3 or A4 paper
6. Felt-tipped pens

REFERENCES
1. Clark , Charles Hutchinson. The Dynamic New Way to Create Successful Ideas Publisher: Classic Business Bookshelf (November 23, 2010) ISBN-10: 1608425614 ISBN-13: 978-1608425617
2. Rawlinson J. Geoffrey Creative Thinking and Brainstorming. Jaico Publishing House (April 30, 2005) ISBN-10: 8172243480 ISBN-13: 978-8172243487

WHEN TO USE THIS METHOD
1. Explore Concepts

HOW TO USE THIS METHOD
1. The moderator introduces the method
2. Break the large group into smaller groups of 3 to 5 people.
3. Supply each group with the materials listed under "resources"
4. Each participant cuts out 10 pictures that they like
5. Each group creates 2 or 3 greeting cards with their own message using the images and materials.
6. Each group presents their cards to the larger group.
7. The moderator introduces a problem statement and the groups use their cards to stimulate ideas for solutions.
8. Pass cards to next group and repeat.
9. When this process is complete review all the solutions with the larger group and select preferred directions.

OBJECTS

remote control
button
computer
phone
car
sailboat
camera
television
internet
gps
mp3 player
book

ACTIONS

smell
hear
touch
see
walk
sing
talk
dance
vision
laugh
magic
swim
play
tell a story

heuristic ideation

WHAT IS IT?
Heuristic ideation method is used to create new concepts, ideas, products or solutions.

WHY USE THIS METHOD?
1. To create new connections and insights for products, services and experiences

WHO INVENTED IT?
Couger 1995, McFadzean 1998, McFadzean, Somersall, and Coker 1998, VanGundy 1988

RESOURCES
1. Pens
2. Markers
3. White board or flip chart
4. Dry erase markers

WHEN TO USE THIS METHOD
1. Explore Concepts

HOW TO USE THIS METHOD
1. The group will first make two lists of words
2. Each team member selects three words from the first list and connects each word to a different word in the second list.
3. Each team members develops these ideas into concepts and illustrates or describes each concept on an index card.
4. The index cards are places on a pin board and each concept is briefly described by the team member who generated the idea.
5. The team votes to prioritize the ideas

REFERENCES
1. McFadzean, E. Creativity in MS / OR: Choosing the Appropriate Technique Interfaces 29: 5 September October 1999 (pp 110 122)

idea advocate

WHAT IS IT?

This method involves appointing advocates for ideas that were previously created during a brainstorming session.

WHO INVENTED IT?

Battelle Institute in Frankfurt, Germany

WHY USE THIS METHOD?

1. Idea advocate is a simplified form of the dialectical approach
2. To ensure fair examination of all ideas.
3. To give every presented idea equal chance of being selected.
4. To uncover the positive aspects of ideas

CHALLENGES

1. Consideration should be given to also assigning a devil's advocate for a more balanced assessment of certain proposed ideas.
2. There should be little difference in status amongst the idea advocates.

WHEN TO USE THIS METHOD

1. Explore Concepts

HOW TO USE THIS METHOD

1. The team reviews a list of previously generated ideas.
2. Assign idea advocate roles to:
3. A team member who proposed an idea, will implement an idea, or argues for the selection of a design direction.
4. The idea advocates present arguments to the design team on why the idea is the best direction.
5. After the advocates have presented the team votes on their preferred idea.

RESOURCES

1. Pens
2. Markers
3. White board or flip chart
4. Dry erase markers

if i were you

WHAT IS IT?
This is a method used to explore scenarios based on methods used by actors that allows refinement of ideas by a design team.

WHO INVENTED IT?
Gerber, E 2009

WHY USE THIS METHOD?
1. Does not require a lot of training.
2. Can take ideas into new areas.

CHALLENGES
1. Needs good moderator.

WHEN TO USE THIS METHOD
1. Know Context
2. Know User
3. Frame insights
4. Explore Concepts

HOW TO USE THIS METHOD
1. Moderator defines scenario.
2. Can use props or empathy tools.
3. Can videotape session.
4. Group sits around a table or on chairs in a circle.
5. Moderator introduces idea or scenario. Each participant in turn adds something to the idea prefixed by the statement "If I was you I would."
6. Statements should be positive

inside the box

WHAT IS IT?

Sometimes people have better ideas if they have some constraints. This brainstorming technique uses constraints to help develop new ideas.

WHO INVENTED IT?

Alex Faickney Osborn 1953 is often credited with inventing brainstorming.

WHY USE THIS METHOD?

1. Leverages the diverse experiences of a team.
2. Makes group problem solving fun.
3. Helps build team cohesion.
4. Everyone can participate.

CHALLENGES

1. Groupthink
2. Not enough good ideas
3. Taking turns
4. Freeloading
5. Inhibition
6. Lack of critical thinking
7. A group that is too large competes for attention.

WHEN TO USE THIS METHOD

1. Generate concepts

HOW TO USE THIS METHOD

1. The moderator introduces the method to the group.
2. The problem is defined by the moderator.
3. The larger group is broken down into groups of 4 or 5 participants
4. The moderator assigns a limitation to each group
5. The moderator instructs each group to come up with a number of ideas if the limitation that they have been assigned is the only limitation that they have.
6. Allow 20 minutes to brainstorm ideas.
7. Participants should record one idea on each index card or post-it-note
8. After 20 minutes display the ideas on a wall organized by the limitation given.
9. The ideas are discussed by the group
10. The moderator groups related ideas.
11. Elect favored concepts and prioritize for further development.

RESOURCES

1. Pens
2. Post-it-notes
3. A flip chart
4. White board or wall
5. Refreshments

journey method

WHAT IS IT?

This is a brainstorming method that uses flexible geographic perspectives to look at a design problem.

WHO INVENTED IT?

Alex Faickney Osborn 1953

WHY USE THIS METHOD?

1. Leverages the diverse experiences of a team.
2. Makes group problem solving fun.
3. Helps build team cohesion.
4. Everyone can participate.

CHALLENGES

1. Some ideas that you generate using the tool may be impractical.
2. Best used with other creativity methods

WHEN TO USE THIS METHOD

1. Generate concepts

HOW TO USE THIS METHOD

1. Define a problem
2. Select a diverse design team of 4 to 12 people and a moderator.
3. Ask team how they would deal with the problem if they were in a different place.
4. Analyze results and prioritize.
5. Develop actionable ideas.

RESOURCES

1. Pens
2. Post-it-notes
3. A flip chart
4. White board or wall
5. Refreshments

REFERENCES

1. Clark , Charles Hutchinson. The Dynamic New Way to Create Successful Ideas Publisher: Classic Business Bookshelf (November 23, 2010) ISBN-10: 1608425614 ISBN-13: 978-1608425617
2. Rawlinson J. Geoffrey Creative Thinking and Brainstorming. Jaico Publishing House (April 30, 2005) ISBN-10: 8172243480 ISBN-13: 978-8172243487

kj method

WHAT IS IT?

The KJ method is a form of brainstorming. The KJ method places emphasis on the most important ideas. It is one of the seven tools of Japanese quality management and incorporates the Buddhist value of structured meditation.

WHO INVENTED IT?

Kawakita Jiro

WHY USE THIS METHOD?

1. There is a hierarchy of ideas
2. This method generates many ideas.
3. This method highlights the connections between ideas which is the starting point for a design solution.

CHALLENGES

1. Groupthink
2. Not enough good ideas
3. Taking turns
4. Freeloading
5. Inhibition
6. Lack of critical thinking
7. A group that is too large competes for attention.

RESOURCES

1. Paper
2. Pens
3. White board
4. Dry-erase markers
5. Post-it-notes.

WHEN TO USE THIS METHOD

1. Explore Concepts

HOW TO USE THIS METHOD

1. The moderator frames the design challenge.
2. Team members generate ideas in up to 25 words on post-it notes.
3. Cards are shuffled and then handed out again to the participants.
4. Each participant should not gat any of their own cards back.
5. Each post-it note is read out by the participants, and all participants review the post-it notes that they hold to find any that seem to go with the one read out, so building a 'group'.
6. Organise post-it notes into groups.
7. Group the groups until you have no more than ten groups.
8. Sort categories into subcategories of 20-30 cards.
9. Refine groups into 10 post-it notes or less.
10. Use a white board or smooth wall.
11. Write the individual post-it notes arranged in groups on the white board or arrange the post-it notes on a wall.
12. The moderator will read out the groups and record the participant's ideas about the relationships and meaning of the information gathered.

A1	A2	A3	B1	B2	B3	C1	C2	C3
A4	**A**	A5	B4	**B**	B5	C4	**C**	C5
A6	A7	A8	B6	B7	B8	C6	C7	C8
D1	D2	D3	A	B	C	E1	E2	E3
D4	**D**	D5	D	■	E	E4	**E**	E5
D6	D7	D8	F	G	H	E6	E7	E8
F1	F2	F3	G1	G2	G3	H1	H2	H3
F4	**F**	F5	G4	**G**	G5	H4	**H**	H5
F6	F7	F8	G6	G7	G8	H6	H7	H8

lotus blossom

WHAT IS IT?

The lotus blossom is a creativity technique that consists a framework for idea generation that starts by generating eight concept themes based on a central theme. Each concept then serves as the basis for eight further theme explorations or variations.

WHO INVENTED IT?

Yasuo Matsumura, Director of the Clover Management Research

WHY USE THIS METHOD?

1. There is a hierarchy of ideas
2. This method requires that a quantity of ideas is generated.
3. shifts you from reacting to a static snapshot of the problem and broadens your perspective toward the problem and the relationships and connections between its components

CHALLENGES

1. It is a somewhat rigid model. Not every problem will require the same number of concepts to be developed.

WHEN TO USE THIS METHOD

1. Explore Concepts

HOW TO USE THIS METHOD

1. Draw up a lotus blossom diagram made up of a square in the center of the diagram and eight circles surrounding the square;
2. Write the problem in the center box of the diagram.
3. Write eight related ideas around the center.
4. Each idea then becomes the central idea of a new theme or blossom.
5. Follow step 3 with all central ideas.

RESOURCES

1. Paper
2. Pens
3. White board
4. Dry-erase markers
5. Post-it-notes.

REFERENCES

1. Michalko M., Thinkpak, Berkeley, California, Ten Speed Press, 1994.
2. Michalko, Michael, Thinkertoys: A handbook of creative-thinking techniques, Second Edition, Ten Speed Press, 2006, Toronto;
3. Sloane, Paul. The Leader's Guide to Lateral Thinking Skills: Unlocking the Creativity and Innovation in You and Your Team (Paperback – 3 Sep 2006);

low fidelity prototyping

WHAT IS IT?

Cardboard prototyping is a quick and cheap way of gaining insight and informing decision making without the need for costly investment. Simulates function but not aesthetics of proposed design. Prototypes help compare alternatives and help answer questions about interactions or experiences.

WHY USE THIS METHOD?

1. May provide the proof of concept
2. It is physical and visible
3. Inexpensive and fast.
4. Useful for refining functional and perceptual interactions.
5. Assists to identify any problems with the design.
6. Helps to reduce the risks
7. Helps members of team to be in alignment on an idea.
8. Helps make abstract ideas concrete.
9. Feedback can be gained from the user

CHALLENGES

1. Producer might get too attached to prototype and it becomes jewelry because it is beautiful rather than a design tool.

WHEN TO USE THIS METHOD

1. Know Context
2. Know User
3. Frame insights
4. Explore Concepts

Image Copyright Liudmila P. Sundikova, 2013
Used under license from Shutterstock.com

HOW TO USE THIS METHOD

1. Construct models, not illustrations
2. Select the important tasks, interactions or experiences to be prototyped.
3. Build to understand problems.
4. If it is beautiful you have invested too much.
5. Make it simple
6. Assemble a kit of inexpensive materials
7. Preparing for a test
8. Select users
9. Conduct test
10. Record notes on the 8x5 cards.
11. Evaluate the results
12. Iterate

RESOURCES

1. Paper
2. Cardboard
3. Wire
4. Foam board,
5. Post-it-notes
6. Hot melt glue

REFERENCES

1. Sefelin, R., Tscheligi, M., & Gukker, V. (2003). Paper Prototyping What is it good for? A Comparison of paper and Computer based Low fidelity Prototyping, CHI 2003, 778-779
2. Snyder, Carolyn (2003). Paper Prototyping: the fast and easy way to design and refine user interfaces. San Francisco, CA: Morgan Kaufmann

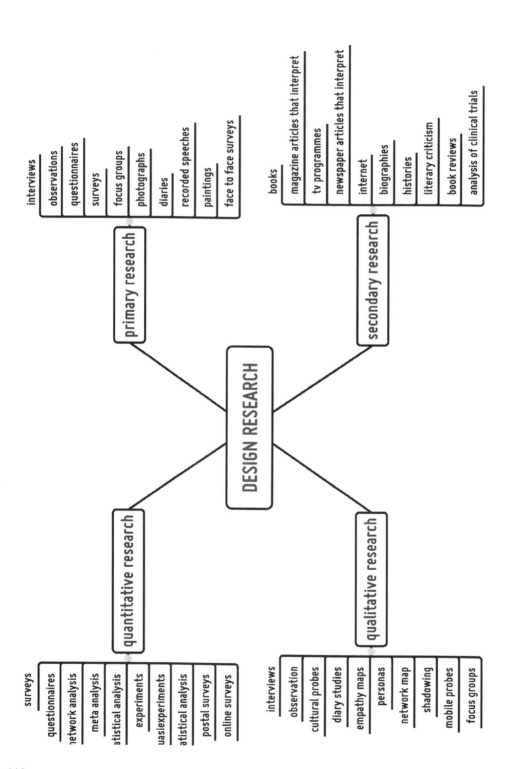

DESIGN RESEARCH

primary research
- interviews
- observations
- questionnaires
- surveys
- focus groups
- photographs
- diaries
- recorded speeches
- paintings
- face to face surveys

secondary research
- books
- magazine articles that interpret
- tv programmes
- newspaper articles that interpret
- internet
- biographies
- histories
- literary criticism
- book reviews
- analysis of clinical trials

quantitative research
- surveys
- questionnaires
- network analysis
- meta analysis
- atistical analysis
- experiments
- uasiexperiments
- atistical analysis
- postal surveys
- online surveys

qualitative research
- interviews
- observation
- cultural probes
- diary studies
- empathy maps
- personas
- network map
- shadowing
- mobile probes
- focus groups

112

mind map

WHAT IS IT?

A mind map is a diagram used to represent the affinities or connections between a number of ideas or things. Understanding connections is the starting point for design. Mind maps are a method of analyzing information and relationships.

WHO INVENTED IT?

Porphry of Tyros 3rd century BC.
Allan Collins, Northwestern University 1960, USA

WHY USE THIS METHOD?

1. The method helps identify relationships.
2. There is no right or wrong with mind maps. They help with they help with memory and organization.
3. Problem solving and brainstorming
4. Relationship discovery
5. Summarizing information
6. Memorizing information

CHALLENGES

Print words clearly, use color and images for visual impact.

WHEN TO USE THIS METHOD

7. Know Context
8. Know User
9. Frame insights
10. Explore Concepts
11. Make Plans

HOW TO USE THIS METHOD

1. Start in the center with a key word or idea. Put box around this node.
2. Use images, symbols, or words for nodes.
3. Select key words.
4. Keep the key word names of nodes s simple and short as possible.
5. Associated nodes should be connected with lines to show affinities.
6. Make the lines the same length as the word/image they support.
7. Use emphasis such as thicker lines to show the strength of associations in your mind map.
8. Use radial arrangement of nodes.

RESOURCES

1. Paper
2. Pens
3. White board
4. Dry-erase markers

REFERENCES

1. Mind maps as active learning tools', by Willis, CL. Journal of computing sciences in colleges. ISSN: 1937-4771. 2006. Volume: 21 Issue: 4
2. Mind Maps as Classroom Exercises John W. Budd The Journal of Economic Education, Vol. 35, No. 1 (Winter, 2004), pp. 35-46 Published by: Taylor & Francis, Ltd.

misuse scenarios

WHAT IS IT?
This is a method that focuses on possible misuse, both unintentional and malicious, of a product or service. The method involves use of scenarios and personas to envision possible misuse cases. These may be:
1. Typical scenarios
2. Atypical scenarios
3. Extreme scenarios

WHO INVENTED IT?
Ian Alexander 2003

WHY USE THIS METHOD?
1. Considering misuse reduces the possibility that a product will fail in use.
2. Consider on projects where there is potential for misuse.
3. High volume manufactured products have high potential for misuse.

CHALLENGES
1. Use customer service feedback to construct misuse scenarios.
2. It is sometimes hard to envision misuse scenarios for new products.

WHEN TO USE THIS METHOD
1. Know Context
2. Know User
3. Frame insights
4. Explore Concepts

HOW TO USE THIS METHOD
1. Think of various types of scenarios and when they may become misuse scenarios.
2. Talk to experts and ask them to provide scenarios of misuse.
3. Consider the context of use and how that may influence misuse.
4. Brainstorm with team to create scenarios of misuse.
5. Create a list of misuse scenarios.
6. Brainstorm remedies for misuse and modify design to remedy misuse.

RESOURCES
1. Pen
2. Paper
3. White board
4. Dry-erase markers
5. Camera

REFERENCES
1. Alexander, Ian, Use/Misuse Case Analysis Elicits Non-Functional Requirements, Computing & Control Engineering Journal, Vol 14, 1, pp 40-45, February 2003
2. Sindre, Guttorm and Andreas L. Opdahl, Templates for Misuse Case Description, Proc. 7th Intl Workshop on Requirements Engineering, Foundation for Software Quality (REFSQ'2001), Interlaken, Switzerland, 4-5 June 2001

Photo: photocase.com - kallejipp

merlin

WHAT IS IT?
The merlin method is a brainstorming method that seeks to develop ideas for improving a product, service or experience by imagining changes in size use or function.

WHY USE THIS METHOD?
1. There is a hierarchy of ideas
2. This method generates many ideas.
3. This method highlights the connections between ideas which is the starting point for design solutions.

WHO INVENTED IT?
Alex Faickney Osborn 1953

CHALLENGES
1. Groupthink
2. Not enough good ideas
3. Taking turns
4. Freeloading
5. Inhibition
6. Lack of critical thinking
7. A group that is too large competes for attention.

WHEN TO USE THIS METHOD
1. Explore Concepts

HOW TO USE THIS METHOD
1. The moderator frames the design challenge.
2. On a whiteboard or flipchart write four headings: enlarge reduce eliminate, reverse.
3. Work for ten minutes with your team under each heading
4. Review the lists, create hierarchy of solutions.

RESOURCES
1. Paper
2. Pens
3. White board
4. Dry-erase markers
5. Post-it-notes.

REFERENCES
1. Clark , Charles Hutchinson. The Dynamic New Way to Create Successful Ideas Publisher: Classic Business Bookshelf (November 23, 2010) ISBN-10: 1608425614 ISBN-13: 978-1608425617
2. Rawlinson J. Geoffrey Creative Thinking and Brainstorming. Jaico Publishing House (April 30, 2005) ISBN-10: 8172243480 ISBN-13: 978-8172243487

nhk method

WHAT IS IT?

The NHK method is a rigorous iterative process of brainstorming of ideas following a predetermined structure.

WHO INVENTED IT?

Hiroshi Takahashi

WHY USE THIS METHOD?

1. This method requires that a quantity of ideas is generated.

CHALLENGES

1. Groupthink
2. Not enough good ideas
3. Taking turns
4. Freeloading
5. Inhibition
6. Lack of critical thinking
7. A group that is too large competes for attention.

WHEN TO USE THIS METHOD

1. Explore Concepts

RESOURCES

1. Paper
2. Pens
3. White board
4. Dry-erase markers
5. Post-it-notes.

HOW TO USE THIS METHOD

1. Define problem statement.
1. Each participant writes down five ideas on five separate cards.
2. Create groups of five participants
3. While each person explains their ideas, the others continue to record new ideas.
4. Collect, and create groups of related concepts.
5. Form new groups of two or three people Brainstorm for half an hour.
6. Groups organize ideas and present them to the larger group.
7. Record all ideas on the white board.
8. Form larger groups of ten people and work further brainstorm each of the ideas on the white board.

REFERENCES

1. Clark , Charles Hutchinson. The Dynamic New Way to Create Successful Ideas Publisher: Classic Business Bookshelf (November 23, 2010) ISBN-10: 1608425614 ISBN-13: 978-1608425617
2. Rawlinson J. Geoffrey Creative Thinking and Brainstorming. Jaico Publishing House (April 30, 2005) ISBN-10: 8172243480 ISBN-13: 978-8172243487

nominal group method

WHAT IS IT?

The nominal group method is a brainstorming method that is designed to encourage participation of all members of the team and minimizes the possibility of more vocal members from dominating the discussion.

WHO INVENTED IT?

William Fox

WHY USE THIS METHOD?

1. To define and prioritize problems or opportunities
2. To understand the best solution to a problem
3. To create a plan to implement an opportunity

RESOURCES

1. White board
2. Dry erase markers
3. Blank postcards

WHEN TO USE THIS METHOD

4. Frame insights
5. Explore Concepts

REFERENCES

1. The Memory Jogger II: A Pocket Guide of Tools for Continuous Improvement and Effective Planning Michael Brassard (Author), Diane Ritter (Author), Francine Oddo (Editor) 1st edition (January 15, 1994) ISBN-10: 1879364441 ISBN-13: 978-1879364448

HOW TO USE THIS METHOD

1. Distribute information about the process to participants before the meeting.
2. Participants drop anonymous suggestions into an unmonitored suggestion box written on blank postcards.
3. The suggestions are distributed to participants before the meeting so that they can think about them.
4. In the meeting the moderator writes the suggestions on to a white board
5. Each participant has the opportunity to speak in support or against any of the suggestions.
6. The moderator leads the team in to clarify each idea,
7. The moderator instructs each person to work silently and independently for five minutes, recording as many ideas, thoughts, or answers as possible on paper.
8. The moderator asks the group to list 5 to 10 ideas that the like the most, in order of importance, and to pass them to the moderator.
9. The moderator counts up the number of votes for each idea.
10. Each participant is given a number of votes that they record on blank postcards which are collected face down and tallied.

nyaka

WHAT IS IT?

The Nyaka method is a form of brainstorming. The Nyaka method places emphasis on exploring problems and solutions to problems.

WHY USE THIS METHOD?

1. There is a hierarchy of ideas
2. This method generates many ideas.

CHALLENGES

1. Groupthink
2. Not enough good ideas
3. Taking turns
4. Freeloading
5. Inhibition
6. Lack of critical thinking
7. A group that is too large competes for attention.

RESOURCES

1. Paper
2. Pens
3. White board
4. Dry-erase markers
5. Post-it-notes.

WHEN TO USE THIS METHOD

1. Explore Concepts

HOW TO USE THIS METHOD

1. Define a moderator
2. The moderator draws a vertical line on a whiteboard.
3. Time limit of 30 minutes
4. The moderator asks the team to define as many things that are wrong with a design or service or experience as possible.
5. The moderator asks the team to define solutions for as many of the problems defined as possible.
6. Create a hierarchy of problems and a hierarchy of solutions for each problem.
7. A group size of 4 to 20 people is optimum.
8. For larger groups the moderator can break the group into groups of 4 or 5 people.

REFERENCES

1. Clark , Charles Hutchinson. The Dynamic New Way to Create Successful Ideas Publisher: Classic Business Bookshelf (November 23, 2010) ISBN-10: 1608425614 ISBN-13: 978-1608425617
2. Rawlinson J. Geoffrey Creative Thinking and Brainstorming. Jaico Publishing House (April 30, 2005) ISBN-10: 8172243480 ISBN-13: 978-8172243487

objectstorming

WHAT IS IT?
A brainstorming technique that uses found objects for inspiration.

WHO INVENTED IT?
Alex Faickney Osborn 1953 is often credited with inventing brainstorming.

WHY USE THIS METHOD?
1. Leverages the diverse experiences of a team.
2. Makes group problem solving fun.
3. Helps build team cohesion.
4. Everyone can participate.

CHALLENGES
1. Groupthink
2. Not enough good ideas
3. Taking turns
4. Freeloading
5. Inhibition
6. Lack of critical thinking
7. A group that is too large competes for attention.

WHEN TO USE THIS METHOD
1. Generate concepts

HOW TO USE THIS METHOD
1. The moderator introduces the method to the group.
2. The problem is defined by the moderator.
3. The larger group is broken down into groups of 4 or 5 participants. The moderator collects a diverse collection of objects before the brainstorming session.
4. Each participant is given two objects and asked to use them as inspiration to generate 10 ideas
5. Allow 20 minutes
6. The participants are asked to vote for their three preferred solutions.
7. Select the top ideas for further development.

RESOURCES
1. Pens
2. Post-it-notes
3. A flip chart
4. White board or wall
5. Refreshments

out of the box

WHAT IS IT?
This is a method to perform out-of-the box brainstorming to generate outrageous and wild ideas.

WHY USE THIS METHOD?
1. To generate wild ideas
2. To promote creative thinking among participants.

RESOURCES
1. Pen
2. Paper
3. White board
4. Dry erase markers
5. Post-it-notes

CHALLENGES
1. Avoid persona representations that may be harmful.
2. Groupthink
3. Not enough good ideas
4. Taking turns
5. Freeloading
6. Inhibition
7. Lack of critical thinking
8. A group that is too large competes for attention.

WHEN TO USE THIS METHOD
1. Explore Concepts

HOW TO USE THIS METHOD
1. The moderator introduces this method.
2. The moderator shows the team several wild or out of the box ideas.
3. Participants generate concepts stressing that they must be wild and out of the box.
4. The moderator records the ideas on a white board.
5. The team reviews the ideas and selects some for further development and bringing back to reality.

RESOURCES
1. Pen
2. Paper
3. White board
4. Dry erase markers
5. Post-it-notes

REFERENCES
1. Clark , Charles Hutchinson. The Dynamic New Way to Create Successful Ideas Publisher: Classic Business Bookshelf (November 23, 2010) ISBN-10: 1608425614 ISBN-13: 978-1608425617
2. Rawlinson J. Geoffrey Creative Thinking and Brainstorming. Jaico Publishing House (April 30, 2005) ISBN-10: 8172243480 ISBN-13: 978-8172243487

pattern language

WHAT IS IT?

Pattern language is an approach to design that uses visual icons rather than words to stimulate and develop design concepts. Developed by Alexander to discover the design factors such as life, wholeness or spirit for architectural projects that he called design elements that give a community "the quality that has no name"

WHO INVENTED IT?

Christopher Alexander, Sara Ishikawa, Murray Silverstein 1977

WHY USE THIS METHOD?

1.   A non verbal approach to design.

RESOURCES

1.   Blank Index cards
2.   Pens
3.   Paper

Image Copyright VOOK, 2013
Used under license from Shutterstock.com

WHEN TO USE THIS METHOD

1.   Explore Concepts

HOW TO USE THIS METHOD

1.   Write a list of about 250 words that are attributes or factors of your design problem.
2.   Create a series of iconic images to illustrate each word on a deck of blank index cards.
3.   Write the associated word on the back face of each icon card.
4.   Spread the cards on a table with the icons facing upwards and randomly associate two or three cards at a time.
5.   Generate concepts based on these associations.
6.   Review the ideas with your team
7.   Prioritize the ideas.
8.   Develop preferred ideas.

REFERENCES

1.   Alexander, C., Ishikawa, S., Silverstein, Murray. (1977). A pattern language. New York: Oxford University Press.

personal

WHAT IS IT?

Recent research has suggested that some individuals are more creative working alone for brainstorming sessions rather than in groups. In this case the divergent idea generation is done by an individual and the convergent phase is done by the team.

WHO INVENTED IT?

Alex Faickney Osborn 1953

WHY USE THIS METHOD?

1. Leverages the diverse experiences of a team.
2. Uses the creativity of the individual free from distractions.
3. Helps build empathy.

CHALLENGES

1. Some ideas that you generate using the tool may be impractical.
2. Best used with other creativity methods

WHEN TO USE THIS METHOD

1. Generate concepts

HOW TO USE THIS METHOD

1. Define a problem
2. Find a quiet place
3. Generate as many ideas as possible in 30 minutes.
4. Get the team together and present the ideas to them.
5. Get the team to vote on which ideas they like the most. Two votes per person.
6. Analyze results and prioritize.
7. Develop actionable ideas.

RESOURCES

1. Pens
2. Post-it-notes
3. A flip chart
4. White board or wall
5. Refreshments

REFERENCES

1. Clark , Charles Hutchinson. The Dynamic New Way to Create Successful Ideas Publisher: Classic Business Bookshelf (November 23, 2010) ISBN-10: 1608425614 ISBN-13: 978-1608425617
2. Rawlinson J. Geoffrey Creative Thinking and Brainstorming. Jaico Publishing House (April 30, 2005) ISBN-10: 8172243480 ISBN-13: 978-8172243487

persona brainstorming

WHAT IS IT?

This is a brainstorming method that uses the imagined perspectives of an identified persona or group identified as one of your client's customer groups such as students look at a design problem.

WHO INVENTED IT?

Alex Faickney Osborn 1953

WHY USE THIS METHOD?

1. Leverages the diverse experiences of a team.
2. Helps build empathy.
3. Makes group problem solving fun.
4. Helps build team cohesion.
5. Everyone can participate.

CHALLENGES

1. Some ideas that you generate using the tool may be impractical.
2. Best used with other creativity methods

WHEN TO USE THIS METHOD

1. Generate concepts

HOW TO USE THIS METHOD

1. Define a problem
2. Select a diverse design team of 4 to 12 people and a moderator.
3. Identify a persona to focus on. See personas.
4. Ask the team how they would deal with the problem if they were the persona
5. Analyze results and prioritize.
6. Develop actionable ideas.

RESOURCES

1. Pens
2. Post-it-notes
3. A flip chart
4. White board or wall
5. Refreshments

REFERENCES

1. Clark , Charles Hutchinson. The Dynamic New Way to Create Successful Ideas Publisher: Classic Business Bookshelf (November 23, 2010) ISBN-10: 1608425614 ISBN-13: 978-1608425617
2. Rawlinson J. Geoffrey Creative Thinking and Brainstorming. Jaico Publishing House (April 30, 2005) ISBN-10: 8172243480 ISBN-13: 978-8172243487

phillips 66 method

WHAT IS IT?

The Phillips 66 method is a method for stimulating interaction such as questions, ideas, or opinions from a large conference group.

WHO INVENTED IT?

Donald Phillips

WHY USE THIS METHOD?

1. Involves a large number of people in a process to share ideas.
2. May generate a large number of ideas.

CHALLENGES

1. The original Phillips 66 process called for the dividing of a large group into groups of 6 people each and to allow 6 minutes per small group for discussing a problem or generating ideas.
2. The small group size should be adjusted to suite the size of the larger group and the discussion time should be adjusted to suite the problem being addressed
3. Two or more teams will generate the same idea through different methods of reasoning.

WHEN TO USE THIS METHOD

1. Explore Concepts

HOW TO USE THIS METHOD

1. Divide the larger group into smaller groups of between 4 and 8 people.
2. The moderator presents a clearly defined problem to all of the groups.
3. Each smaller group should move to an area where they can discuss the problem.
4. Each small group should select a spokesperson to record and later present their conclusions.
5. Each group should discuss the problem for between 6 and 30 minutes.
6. The group spokesperson records the ideas.
7. Each group selects the top one to three ideas. The number selected depends on time available for the presentations to the larger group.
8. The selected ideas are recorded and passed on to the moderator. This can be done using index cards.
9. The selected ideas are reviewed by the moderator and discussed by the larger group or reviewed and discussed at a later time.

RESOURCES

1. Pens
2. Index cards
3. Post-it-notes
4. White board
5. Dry erase markers

pictive

1. WHAT IS IT?

PICTIVE (Plastic Interface for Collaborative Technology Initiative through Video Exploration) is a low fidelity participatory design method used to develop graphical user interfaces. It allows users to participate in the development process. A PICTIVE prototype gives a user a sense of what a system or a piece of software will look like and how it will behave when completed.

WHO INVENTED IT?

Developed by Michael J. Muller and others at Bell Communications Research around 1990

WHY USE THIS METHOD?

2. Less development time.
3. Less development costs.
4. Involves users.
5. Gives quantifiable user feedback.
6. Facilitates system implementation since users know what to expect.
7. Results user oriented solutions.
8. Gets users with diverse experience involved.

CHALLENGES

1. Designers can become too attached to their prototypes and allow them to become jewelry that stands in the way of further refinement.
2. Don't worry about it being pretty.

WHEN TO USE THIS METHOD

1. Explore Concepts

HOW TO USE THIS METHOD

1. A PICTIVE is usually made from simple available tools and materials like pens, paper, Post-It stickers, paper clips and icons on cards.
2. Allow thirty minutes for initial design.
3. Allow ten minutes for user testing.
4. Ten minutes for modification.
5. Five minutes for user testing.
6. Create task scenario.
7. Anything that moves or changes should be a separate element.
8. The designer uses these materials to represent elements such as drop-down boxes, menu bars, and special icons. During a design session, users modify the mock up based on their own experience.
9. Take notes for later review.
10. Record the session with a video camera
11. The team then reviews the ideas and develops a strategy to apply them.
12. A PICTIVE enables non technical people to participate in the design process.

REFERENCES

1. Michael J. Muller PICTIVE an exploration in participatory design. Published in: · Proceeding CHI '91 Proceedings of the SIGCHI Conference on Human Factors in Computing Systems Pages 225-231 ACM New York, NY, USA ©1991 table of contents ISBN:0-89791-383-3 doi 10.1145/108844.108896

pin cards

WHAT IS IT?

The pin cards technique is a brainwriting process to generate ideas on colored cards that are sorted into groups and discussed. This method allows participants to think of more ideas during the writing process. This method can generate more ideas than some other brainstorming methods.

WHO INVENTED IT?

Wolfgang Schnelle

WHY USE THIS METHOD?

1. To generate ideas to solve a problem
2. To produce many ideas quickly and without filtering from other participants.

CHALLENGES

1. Cards need to be passed on quickly
2. Participants may feel time stressed.
3. Some participants may want to make their ideas confidential.

RESOURCES

1. Colored blank index cards
2. Pins
3. Pin Board
4. Pens
5. Markers

WHEN TO USE THIS METHOD

1. Explore Concepts

HOW TO USE THIS METHOD

1. The moderator writes the problem statement on a white board.
2. The participants should be seated around a large table.
3. The moderator distributes 10 cards of the same color to each participant.
4. Each participant receives different-colored cards.
5. Participants record one idea per card.
6. Ideas can be a cartoon sketch or a sentence
7. Completed cards are passed to the person on the participant's right hand side.
8. Participants can review cards from a person on their left hand side.
9. After 30 to 45 minutes all the participants pin the cards that they have to a wall.
10. Each participant should aim to produce at least 40 ideas.
11. The team sorts the cards into a number of groups by association. The type of association are determined by the group.
12. The participants prioritize the groups and combine the ideas in the favored group for further development.

REFERENCES

1. Nancy R. Tague .The Quality Toolbox, Second Edition. SQ Quality Press; 2 edition (March 30, 2005) ISBN-10: 0873896394 ISBN-13: 978-0873896399

pool method

WHAT IS IT?

Brainstorming is one of the oldest, fastest and most widely used creativity methods. Brainstorming does need to be undertaken by experts. It can be undertaken as a group or individually. Osborn believed that brainstorming as a group was most effective. Recent research has questioned this assumption. It should be used to address a single problem. Brainstorming is worthwhile when it is part of a larger process of design.

WHO INVENTED IT?

Alex Faickney Osborn 1953

WHY USE THIS METHOD?

1. It is useful for generating new types of solutions to problems.
2. It can be used to overcome creative blocks.
3. There is group buy-in to a design direction.

CHALLENGES

1. Groupthink
2. Not enough good ideas
3. Taking turns
4. Freeloading
5. Inhibition
6. Lack of critical thinking
7. A group that is too large competes for attention.

WHEN TO USE THIS METHOD

1. Explore Concepts

HOW TO USE THIS METHOD

1. Define the problem
2. Moderator briefs the design team.
3. A group size of 4 to 20 people is optimum.
4. Supply each team member with a pile of 50 blank index cards
5. Give the team 30 minutes to create 10 ideas each.
6. Each team member describes their ideas and places the cards with the ideas, one per card in a central pool.
7. Give the team another 30 minutes. Each team members can select one or more ideas to develop which have been created by another team member from the central pool to develop in the second session.

post-it

WHAT IS IT?

It is a method that uses combinations of brainstormed words to generate ideas.

WHY USE THIS METHOD?

1.   New ideas start with making new connections.

RESOURCES

1.   Whiteboard
2.   Dry erase markers
3.   Post-it notes
4.   Pens
5.   Paper
6.   Markers

WHEN TO USE THIS METHOD

1.   Explore Concepts

HOW TO USE THIS METHOD

1.   Ask your team to write all the words that they associate with the problem.
2.   One word per post-it-note.
3.   Spread the post-it-notes over a wall.
4.   As the second level of brainstorming generate ideas based on combinations of words
5.   Brainstorm a list of "how to" solutions based on the ideas.

related context

WHAT IS IT?
A method that involves discovering and projecting the thinking of another sector, brand, organization or context onto a design problem.

WHY USE THIS METHOD?
A method of discovering affinities that can facilitate innovative thinking and solutions.
1. Scenarios become a focus for discussion which helps evaluate and refine concepts.
2. Usability issues can be explored.
3. Scenarios help us create an end to end experience.
4. Personas give us a framework to evaluate possible solutions.

CHALLENGES
1. Strong personalities can influence the group in negative ways.
2. Include problem situations
3. Hard to envision misuse scenarios.

WHEN TO USE THIS METHOD
1. Know Context
2. Know User
3. Frame insights
4. Generate Concepts

HOW TO USE THIS METHOD
1. Identify a design problem
2. Put together a design team of 4 to 12 members with a moderator.
3. Brainstorm a list of sectors, organizations, or contexts that may imply a different approach or thinking to your design problem.
4. Imagine your design problem with the associated list.
5. Generate concepts for each relationship
6. Vote for favored directions using dot voting method.
7. Analyze and summarize insights.

RESOURCES
1. Post-it notes
2. White board
3. Paper
4. Pens
5. Dry-erase markers

REFERENCES
1. "Scenarios," IDEO Method Cards. ISBN 0-9544132-1-0
2. Carroll, John M. Making Use: Scenario-based design of human-computer interactions. MIT Press, 2000.
3. Carroll J. M. Five Reasons for Scenario Based Design. Elsevier Science B. V. 2000.

resources

WHAT IS IT?
This is a brainstorming method that uses the availability of resources to look at a design problem.

WHO INVENTED IT?
Alex Faickney Osborn 1953

WHY USE THIS METHOD?
1. Leverages the diverse experiences of a team.
2. Helps build empathy.
3. Makes group problem solving fun.
4. Helps build team cohesion.
5. Everyone can participate.

CHALLENGES
1. Some ideas that you generate using the tool may be impractical.
2. Best used with other creativity methods

REFERENCES
1. Clark , Charles Hutchinson. The Dynamic New Way to Create Successful Ideas Publisher: Classic Business Bookshelf (November 23, 2010) ISBN-10: 1608425614 ISBN-13: 978-1608425617
2. Rawlinson J. Geoffrey Creative Thinking and Brainstorming. Jaico Publishing House (April 30, 2005) ISBN-10: 8172243480 ISBN-13: 978-8172243487

WHEN TO USE THIS METHOD
1. Generate concepts

HOW TO USE THIS METHOD
1. Define a problem
2. Select a diverse design team of 4 to 12 people and a moderator.
3. Identify a resource to limit or make more available such as finance, time, people, materials or process.
4. Ask the team how they would deal with the problem if the resource was changed as proposed
5. Analyze results and prioritize.
6. Develop actionable ideas.

RESOURCES
1. Pens
2. Post-it-notes
3. A flip chart
4. White board or wall
5. Refreshments

rolestorming

WHAT IS IT?
Rolestorming is a brainstorming method where participants adopt other people's identity while brainstorming.

WHO INVENTED IT?
Rick Griggs1980s

WHY USE THIS METHOD?
1. Helps reduce inhibitions which some team members may have in suggesting innovative solutions.

CHALLENGES
1. Avoid persona representations that may be harmful.
2. Groupthink
3. Not enough good ideas
4. Taking turns
5. Freeloading
6. Inhibition
7. Lack of critical thinking
8. A group that is too large competes for attention.

WHEN TO USE THIS METHOD
1. Explore Concepts

HOW TO USE THIS METHOD
1. Select moderator
2. Conduct a traditional brainstorming session
3. At the conclusion of the first brainstorming session the moderator identifies a number of identities to be used for the second session
4. The identities can be any person not in the brainstorming group such as a competitor, a famous person, a boss. They should be known to the team members.
5. The Moderator asks some questions
How would this identity solve the problem?
What would this persona see as the problem?
Where would this persona see the problem?
Why would the persona see a problem?
6. Brainstorm in character.
7. Use words such as "My persona"
8. Share ideas.

REFERENCES
1. Clark , Charles Hutchinson. The Dynamic New Way to Create Successful Ideas Publisher: Classic Business Bookshelf (November 23, 2010) ISBN-10: 1608425614 ISBN-13: 978-1608425617
2. Rawlinson J. Geoffrey Creative Thinking and Brainstorming. Jaico Publishing House (April 30, 2005) ISBN-10: 8172243480 ISBN-13: 978-8172243487

sensorial method

WHAT IS IT?

Design in northern Europe and the United States focuses on the visual sense which is only a component of the design experience. A design such as an Italian sports car gives greater consideration to other senses such as hearing, smell touch to give a consistent experience of through all senses to a product user.

WHO INVENTED IT?

Rob Curedale 1995

WHY USE THIS METHOD?

1. It gives a design a greater experience of quality than a design that focuses on the visual sense.
2. It gives a consistent experience.
3. It provides a more stimulating experience than a design that focuses on the visual experience.

CHALLENGES

1. Groupthink
2. Not enough good ideas
3. Taking turns
4. Freeloading
5. Inhibition
6. Lack of critical thinking
7. A group that is too large competes for attention.

WHEN TO USE THIS METHOD

1. Explore Concepts

HOW TO USE THIS METHOD

1. The moderator frames the design challenge.
2. Team members generate ideas on post-it notes.
3. The team works through 20 minute brainstorming sessions in each sense, Vision, smell, touch hearing, taste.
4. Ask team members to generate 6 to 10 ideas each under each category.
5. Use up to 25 words for non visual senses and simple sketches for the visual ideas.
6. Organise post-it notes into groups through discussion with five concepts in each group, one idea from each sense group or five different senses in each group.
7. Ask team to vote on which groups have the most potential for further development.

RESOURCES

1. Paper
2. Pens
3. White board
4. Dry-erase markers
5. Post-it-notes.

scenarios

WHAT IS IT?

A scenario is a narrative or story about how people may experience a design in a particular future context of use. They can be used to predict or explore future interactions with concept products or services. Scenarios can be presented by media such as storyboards or video or be written. They can feature single or multiple actors participating in product or service interactions.

WHO INVENTED IT?

Herman Kahn, Rand Corporation 1950, USA

WHY USE THIS METHOD?

1. Scenarios become a focus for discussion which helps evaluate and refine concepts.
2. Usability issues can be explored at a very early stage in the design process.
3. The are useful tool to align a team vision.
4. Scenarios help us create an end to end experience.
5. Interactive experiences involve the dimension of time.
6. Personas give us a framework to evaluate possible solutions.

CHALLENGES

1. Generate scenarios for a range of situations.
2. Include problem situations
3. Hard to envision misuse scenarios.

WHEN TO USE THIS METHOD

1. Frame insights
2. Generate Concepts
3. Create Solutions

HOW TO USE THIS METHOD

1. Identify the question to investigate.
2. Decide time and scope for the scenario process.
3. Identify stake holders and uncertainties.
4. Define the scenarios.
5. Create storyboards of users goals, activities, motivations and tasks.
6. Act out the scenarios.
7. The session can be videotaped.
8. Analyze the scenarios through discussion.
9. Summarize insights

RESOURCES

1. Storyboard templates
2. Pens
3. Video cameras
4. Props
5. White board
6. Dry-erase markers

REFERENCES

1. "Scenarios," IDEO Method Cards. ISBN 0-9544132-1-0
2. Carroll, John M. Making Use: Scenario-based design of human-computer interactions. MIT Press, 2000.
3. Carroll J. M. Five Reasons for Scenario Based Design. Elsevier Science B. V. 2000.
4. Carroll, John M. Scenario-Based Design: Envisioning Work and Technology in System Development.

WORD LISTS

VERB LIST	ADJECTIVE LIST	ADVERB LIST	PRODUCT LIST
walk	adaptable	accidentally	GPS
stand	adventurous	anxiously	marine
reach	affable	beautifully	printer
sit	affectionate	blindly	copy
jump	agreeable	boldly	chair
fly	ambitious	bravely	sofa
accept	amiable	brightly	video
allow	amicable	calmly	game
advise	amusing	carefully	camera
answer	brave	carelessly	desk
arrive	bright	cautiously	tv
ask	broad-minded	clearly	music
avoid	calm	correctly	floor
stop	careful	courageously	bookcase
agree	charming	cruelly	tools
deliver	communicative	daringly	fence
depend	compassionate	deliberately	cart
describe	conscientious	doubtfully	car
deserve	considerate	eagerly	house
destroy	convivial	easily	bean bag
disappear	courageous	elegantly	audio

semantic intuition

WHAT IS IT?
Semantic intuition is a method of generating ideas based on word associations.

WHO INVENTED IT?
Warfield, Geschka, & Hamilton, 1975. Battelle Institute

WHY USE THIS METHOD?
1.   To find new solutions to a problem.

WHEN TO USE THIS METHOD
1.   Explore Concepts

RESOURCES
1.   Pens
2.   Paper
3.   Post-it –notes
4.   White board
5.   Dry erase markers.

HOW TO USE THIS METHOD
1.   Define the problem to be explored.
2.   The team brainstorms two to four word lists that are related to the problem. They could be for example a list of nouns, a list of verbs and a list of adjectives.
3.   The team makes a forth lists of associations of two or three words from the lists that can form the basis of new ideas.
4.   Combine one word from one set with another word from the other set.
5.   The team visualizes new products services or experiences based on the word associations.
6.   Each team member produces five to ten ideas based on the word associations over a 30 minute period.
7.   The ideas are prioritized by the group by voting.

REFERENCES
1.   Warfield, J. N., H. Geschka, and R. Hamilton, Methods of Idea Management, Approaches to Problem Solving No. 4, Columbus: Academy for Contemporary Problems, August, 1975.

six thinking hats

WHAT IS IT?

Six thinking hats is a tool for thinking described in a book by the same name by Edward de Bono. It can help a design team understand the effects of decisions from different viewpoints.

1. White Hat thinking is information, numbers, data needs and gaps.
2. Red Hat thinking is intuition, desires and emotion.
3. Black Hat thinking is the hat of judgment and care.
4. Yellow Hat thinking is the logical positive.
5. Green Hat thinking is the hat of creativity, alternatives, proposals, provocations and change.
6. Blue Hat thinking is the overview or process control.

WHO INVENTED IT?

Edward de Bono 1985

CHALLENGES

1. When describing your concept, be specific about your goal.
2. Utilize your thinking for practical solutions.
3. Always think in the style of the hat you're wearing.
4. Stick to the rules.

WHY USE THIS METHOD?

The key theoretical reasons to use the Six Thinking Hats are to:

1. Encourage Parallel Thinking
2. Encourage full-spectrum thinking
3. Separate ego from performance
4. Encourage critical thinking.

Image Copyright Olga Popova, 2013 Used under license from Shutterstock.com

WHEN TO USE THIS METHOD

1. Know Context
2. Know User
3. Frame insights
4. Generate Concepts
5. Create Solutions

HOW TO USE THIS METHOD

1. Optimum number of participants is 4 to 8.
2. Present the facts White Hat.
3. Generate ideas on how the issue should be handled Green Hat.
4. Evaluate the ideas. Yellow Hat.
5. List the drawbacks Black Hat.
6. Get the feelings about alternatives Red Hat.
7. Summarize and finish the meeting. Blue Hat.
8. Time required 90 minutes.

RESOURCES

1. Paper and
2. Pens,
3. Descriptions of different hats
4. Symbols of hats
5. Space to sit in the circle

REFERENCES

1. de Bono, Edward (1985). Six Thinking Hats: An Essential Approach to Business Management. Little, Brown, & Company. ISBN 0-316-17791-1 (hardback) and 0316178314 (paperback).
2. Moseley, D., Baumfield, V., Elliott, J., Gregson, M., Higgins, S., Miller, J., Newton, D. (2005). "De Bono's lateral and parallel thinking tools", in ed. Moseley, David: Frameworks for Thinking. Cambridge University Press.

scamper

WHAT IS IT?

SCAMPER is a brainstorming technique and creativity method that uses seven words as prompts.

1. Substitute.
2. Combine.
3. Adapt.
4. Modify.
5. Put to another use.
6. Eliminate.
7. Reverse.

WHO INVENTED IT?

Bob Eberle based on work by Alex Osborne

WHY USE THIS METHOD?

1. Scamper is a method that can help generate innovative solutions to a problem.
2. Leverages the diverse experiences of a team.
3. Makes group problem solving fun.
4. Helps get buy in from all team members for solution chosen.
5. Helps build team cohesion.
6. Everyone can participate.

CHALLENGES

1. Some ideas that you generate using the tool may be impractical.
2. Best used with other creativity methods

SEE ALSO

1. Brainstorming

WHEN TO USE THIS METHOD

1. Generate concepts

HOW TO USE THIS METHOD

1. Select a product or service to apply the method.
2. Select a diverse design team of 4 to 12 people and a moderator.
3. Ask questions about the product you identified, using the SCAMPER mnemonic to guide you.
4. Create as many ideas as you can.
5. Analyze
6. Prioritize.
7. Select the best single or several ideas to further brainstorm.

RESOURCES

1. Pens
2. Post-it-notes
3. A flip chart
4. White board or wall
5. Refreshments

REFERENCES

1. Scamper: Creative Games and Activities for Imagination Development. Bob Eberle April 1, 1997 ISBN-10: 1882664248 ISBN-13: 978-1882664245

SCAMPER QUESTIONS

SUBSTITUTE

1. What materials or resources can you substitute or swap to improve the product?
2. What other product or process could you substitute?
3. What rules could you use?
4. Can you use this product in another situation?

COMBINE

1. Could you combine this product with another product?
2. Could you combine several goals?
3. Could you combine the use of the product with another use?
4. Could you join resources with someone else?

ADAPT

1. How could you adapt or readjust this product to serve another purpose or use?
2. What else is the product like?
3. What could you imitate to adapt this product?
4. What exists that is like the product?
5. Could the product adapt to another context?

MODIFY

1. How could you change the appearance of the product?
2. What could you change ?
3. What could you focus on to create more return on investment?
4. Could you change part of the product?

PUT TO ANOTHER USE

1. Can you use this product in another situation?
2. Who would find this product useful?
3. How would this product function in a new context?
4. Could you recycle parts of this product to create a new product?

ELIMINATE

1. How could you make the product simpler?
2. What features, parts, could you eliminate?
3. What could you understate or tone down?
4. Could you make the product smaller or more efficient?
5. Would the product function differently if you removed part of the product?

REVERSE

1. What would happen if you changed the operation sequence?
2. What if you do the reverse of what you are trying to do?
3. What components could you substitute to change the order of this product?
4. What roles could you change?

STP CHART

SITUATION	TARGET	PROPOSAL

stp method

WHAT IS IT?

STP is a brainstorming method designed to help define ways of reaching a goal.

WHO INVENTED IT?

Ava S Butler 1996

WHY USE THIS METHOD?

1. To generate new ideas

CHALLENGES

1. Groupthink
2. Not enough good ideas
3. Taking turns
4. Freeloading
5. Inhibition
6. Lack of critical thinking
7. A group that is too large competes for attention.

RESOURCES

1. Pens
2. Post-it-notes
3. A flip chart
4. White board or wall
5. Refreshments.

REFERENCES

1. Butler, Ava S. (1996) Teamthink Publisher: Mcgraw Hill ISBN 0070094330
2. Clark, Charles Hutchinson. The Dynamic New Way to Create Successful Ideas Publisher: Classic Business Bookshelf (November 23, 2010) ISBN-10: 1608425614 ISBN-13: 978-1608425617
3. Rawlinson J. Geoffrey Creative Thinking and Brainstorming. Jaico Publishing House (April 30, 2005) ISBN-10: 8172243480

WHEN TO USE THIS METHOD

1. Explore Concepts

HOW TO USE THIS METHOD

1. The moderator writes three headings on a white board. Situation, target and proposal.
2. The moderator reviews the rules of brainstorming. Go for quantity.
3. The moderator asks the question "What do you see as the current situation?"
4. When all ideas have been recorded the moderator asks "Which comments need clarification?"
5. After team members provide clarification the moderator asks " What is our ideal goal?"
6. After all ideas have been recorded and clarifies the moderator asks" What is our preferred target?"
7. After the team votes and a preferred target is selected the moderator asks "How can we get from our current situation to our preferred target?"
8. After all ideas have been recorded and clarified the team selects a preferred way to get to the target by voting.

starbusting

WHAT IS IT?

Starbursting generates questions to clarify issues, probe for potential solutions, or verify resource requirements.

WHO INVENTED IT?

Alex Faickney Osborn 1953

WHY USE THIS METHOD?

1. To identify potential problem areas
2. Useful for generating new types of solutions to problems.

CHALLENGES

1. No evaluation of questions is allowed during the starbursting process.
2. Groupthink
3. Not enough good ideas
4. Taking turns
5. Freeloading
6. Inhibition
7. Lack of critical thinking
8. A group that is too large competes
9. for attention.

RESOURCES

1. Pens
2. Post-it-notes
3. A flip chart
4. White board or wall
5. Refreshments.

WHEN TO USE THIS METHOD

1. Explore Concepts

HOW TO USE THIS METHOD

1. The fist step is to define a problem to be explored or to review a set of previously brainstormed ideas.
2. The participants may ask as many questions as they would like without other participants judging them.
3. Participants write their questions on 3 × 5 inch index cards.
4. The moderator collects the questions and writes them on a white board.
5. The team organizes the questions into related groups and prioritizes them

RESOURCES

1. Pens
2. 3 x5 inch blank index cards
3. White board or wall
4. Refreshments.

REFERENCES

1. Clark , Charles Hutchinson. The Dynamic New Way to Create Successful Ideas Publisher: Classic Business Bookshelf (November 23, 2010) ISBN-10: 1608425614 ISBN-13: 978-1608425617
2. Rawlinson J. Geoffrey Creative Thinking and Brainstorming. Jaico Publishing House (April 30, 2005) ISBN-10: 8172243480 ISBN-13: 978-8172243487

synectics

WHAT IS IT?

Synectics is a structured creativity method that is based on analogy. Synectics is based on ob-servations collected during thousands of hours of group process and group problem solving and decision making activities (Nolan 1989)The word synectics combines derives from Greek "the bringing together of diverse elements."

WHO INVENTED IT?

George Prince and William Gordon 1976

WHY USE THIS METHOD?

1. Use to stimulate creative thinking and generate new problem solving approaches.
2. Synectics provides an environment in which risk taking is validated.
3. Synectics can be fun and productive.

CHALLENGES

1. Synectics is more demanding than brain-storming,
2. If the analogy is too obvious, then it may not promote innovative thinking.
3. Synectics works best as a group process.

WHEN TO USE THIS METHOD

1. Frame insights
2. Generate Concepts

HOW TO USE THIS METHOD

1. Problem definition.
2. Create an analogy. Use ideas from the natural or man-made world, connections with historical events, your location, etc.
3. Use this Sentence Stem: An is a lot like a y because...
4. Use a syntectic trigger Mechanism like a picture, poem, song, drawing etc. to start your analogical reasoning.
5. The group generates as many solution ap-proaches, called springboards, as possible.
6. Idea selection.
7. Excursions – Structured side trips.
8. Develop the selected ideas into concepts.
9. Analyze the connections in the analogy you have created.

RESOURCES

1. Paper
2. Pens
3. White board
4. Dry-erase markers

REFERENCES

1. Gordon, William J.J. Synectics: The Devel-opment of Creative Capacity. (New York: Harper and row, Publishers, 1961
2. Nolan, Vincent. "Whatever Happened to Synectics?" Creativity and Innovation Management, v. 21 n.1 (2003): 25.

thought leader

WHAT IS IT?

This is a brainstorming method that brainstorms imagined solutions that may be proposed by some of the most thoughtful people who have lived.

WHO INVENTED IT?

Alex Faickney Osborn 1953

WHY USE THIS METHOD?

1. Leverages the diverse experiences of a team.
2. Helps build empathy.
3. Makes group problem solving fun.
4. Helps build team cohesion.
5. Everyone can participate.

CHALLENGES

1. Some ideas that you generate using the tool may be impractical.
2. Best used with other creativity methods

REFERENCES

1. Clark , Charles Hutchinson. The Dynamic New Way to Create Successful Ideas Publisher: Classic Business Bookshelf (November 23, 2010) ISBN-10: 1608425614 ISBN-13: 978-1608425617
2. Rawlinson J. Geoffrey Creative Thinking and Brainstorming. Jaico Publishing House (April 30, 2005) ISBN-10: 8172243480 ISBN-13: 978-8172243487

WHEN TO USE THIS METHOD

1. Generate concepts

HOW TO USE THIS METHOD

1. Define a problem
2. Select a diverse design team of 4 to 12 people and a moderator.
3. Identify a thought leader to focus on to explore the solutions such as Steve Jobs, James Dyson, Thomas Edison, Bill Gates, Henry Ford, Steven Spielberg, Albert Einstein, Richard Branson or Leonardo Da Vinci.
4. The moderator asks the group how they imagine that this person may solve the problem.
5. Analyze results and prioritize.
6. Develop actionable ideas.

RESOURCES

1. Pens
2. Post-it-notes
3. A flip chart
4. White board or wall
5. Refreshments

written scenario

WHAT IS IT?
Scenarios are stories that describe a possible future event. Scenarios are used by organizations to understand different ways that future events might unfold

WHO INVENTED THIS METHOD?
Herman Kahn RAND 1950s

WHY USE THIS METHOD?
1. A written scenario helps a designer understand interactions of an intended user with a product service or experience.
2. Scenarios can also be used for evaluating an intened design.

WHEN TO USE THIS METHOD
1. Define intent
2. Know Context
3. Know User
4. Frame insights
5. Explore Concepts
6. Make Plans

CHALLENGES
1. Work in small groups
2. Avoid identifying one solution
3. Keep focussed on the problem.

HOW TO USE THIS METHOD
1. Decide on the key question to be answered.
2. Determine the time and scope of the scenario.
3. Determine the stakeholders or actors.
4. Determine the goals the actor has to complete.
5. Map basic trends and driving forces.
6. Consider key uncertainties.
7. Determine a starting point of the scenario: a trigger or an event.
8. You need to have an understanding of the users and the context of use.
9. Brainstorm possible solutions.
10. Produce 7 to 9 initial mini-scenarios
11. Reduce to 2 to 3 scenarios
12. You can use story boarding.
13. In simple language describe the interactions.
14. Assess the scenarios. Identify the issues arising.

RESOURCES
1. Paper
2. Pens

REFERENCES
1. Schoemaker, Paul J.H. "Scenario Planning: A Tool for Strategic Thinking," Sloan Management Review. Winter: 1995, pp. 25-40.
2. M. Lindgren & H. Bandhold, Scenario planning — the link between future and strategy, Palgrave Macmillan, 2003

time machine

WHAT IS IT?
This is a brainstorming method that uses flexible time perspectives to look at a design problem.

WHO INVENTED IT?
Alex Faickney Osborn 1953

WHY USE THIS METHOD?
1. Leverages the diverse experiences of a team.
2. Makes group problem solving fun.
3. Helps build team cohesion.
4. Everyone can participate.

CHALLENGES
1. Some ideas that you generate using the tool may be impractical.
2. Best used with other creativity methods

REFERENCES
1. Clark , Charles Hutchinson. The Dynamic New Way to Create Successful Ideas Publisher: Classic Business Bookshelf (November 23, 2010) ISBN-10: 1608425614 ISBN-13: 978-1608425617
2. Rawlinson J. Geoffrey Creative Thinking and Brainstorming. Jaico Publishing House (April 30, 2005) ISBN-10: 8172243480 ISBN-13: 978-8172243487

WHEN TO USE THIS METHOD
1. Generate concepts

HOW TO USE THIS METHOD
1. Define a problem
2. Select a diverse design team of 4 to 12 people and a moderator.
3. Ask team how they would deal with the problem if they were living 10 years ago, 1000 years ago, 10,000 years ago?
4. Ask the team how they would dal with the problem if they were living 5 years in the future, ten years, 100 years 1,000 years in the future?
5. Analyze results and prioritize.
6. Develop actionable ideas.

RESOURCES
1. Pens
2. Post-it-notes
3. A flip chart
4. White board or wall
5. Refreshments

trigger method

WHAT IS IT?

Iteration is important at all stages of the design process. This method takes the ideas of an initial brainstorming session and uses these ideas to build upon in a second session.

WHO INVENTED IT?

Alex Faickney Osborn 1953

WHY USE THIS METHOD?

1. Leverages the diverse experiences of a team.
2. Iteration allows refinement or ideas.
3. Makes group problem solving fun.
4. Helps build team cohesion.
5. Everyone can participate.

CHALLENGES

1. Some ideas that you generate using the tool may be impractical.
2. Best used with other creativity methods

REFERENCES

1. Clark , Charles Hutchinson. The Dynamic New Way to Create Successful Ideas Publisher: Classic Business Bookshelf (November 23, 2010) ISBN-10: 1608425614 ISBN-13: 978-1608425617
2. Rawlinson J. Geoffrey Creative Thinking and Brainstorming. Jaico Publishing House (April 30, 2005) ISBN-10: 8172243480 ISBN-13: 978-8172243487

WHEN TO USE THIS METHOD

1. Generate concepts

HOW TO USE THIS METHOD

1. Ideas from a first brainstorming session are presented to the group.
2. The group creates a hierarchy by voting for the favored ideas.
3. The one or 3 ideas are selected as the basis for the brainstorming session.
4. Analyze results and prioritize.
5. Develop actionable ideas.

RESOURCES

1. Pens
2. Post-it-notes
3. A flip chart
4. White board or wall
5. Refreshments

up and down

WHAT IS IT?
This is a brainstorming method that creates ideas from the top and lowest employees of an organization

WHO INVENTED IT?
Alex Faickney Osborn 1953

WHY USE THIS METHOD?
1. It is useful for generating new types of solutions to problems.
2. Brainstorming allows each person in a group to better understand a problem.
3. It can be used to overcome creative blocks.
4. There is group buy-in to a design direction.

CHALLENGES
1. Groupthink
2. Not enough good ideas
3. Taking turns
4. Freeloading
5. Inhibition
6. Lack of critical thinking
7. A group that is too large competes for attention.

WHEN TO USE THIS METHOD
1. Explore Concepts

HOW TO USE THIS METHOD
1. Ask your team to brainstorm the viewpoint of the CEO
2. Ask your team to brainstorm the problem from the viewpoint of the lowest employee
3. How would the problem be different from their perspectives?
4. Formulate how to statements.

RESOURCES
1. Pens
2. Post-it-notes
3. A flip chart
4. White board or wall
5. Refreshments.

REFERENCES
1. Clark , Charles Hutchinson. The Dynamic New Way to Create Successful Ideas Publisher: Classic Business Bookshelf (November 23, 2010) ISBN-10: 1608425614 ISBN-13: 978-1608425617
2. Rawlinson J. Geoffrey Creative Thinking and Brainstorming. Jaico Publishing House (April 30, 2005) ISBN-10: 8172243480 ISBN-13: 978-8172243487

wishful thinking

WHAT IS IT?

This method gives your team members an opportunity to propose possible outcomes that they would like to see and the team to brainstorm each team member's wish.

WHY USE THIS METHOD?

1. It is useful for generating new types of solutions to problems.
2. Brainstorming allows each person in a group to better understand a problem.
3. It can be used to overcome creative blocks.
4. There is group buy-in to a design direction.

CHALLENGES

1. Some team members may find the initial wishes challenging.

WHEN TO USE THIS METHOD

2. Frame insights
3. Explore Concepts

RESOURCES

1. Pens
2. Post-it-notes
3. A flip chart
4. White board or wall
5. Refreshments.

HOW TO USE THIS METHOD

1. Define the problem.
2. Moderator provides an overview of the method.
3. The participants each generate one wish. An example may be : 'We should have more flexible work hours"
4. The moderator records the statements on a white board
5. In a second stage of the brainstorm which can be called "reality check" The participants review the wish list and suggest how each wish may be actualized in a practical way. Ask: "How can we really do this?" "What resource could be used?" "What could happen if we try this?"
6. The team reviews the second list and votes on their preferred directions for further development.

REFERENCES

1. Clark , Charles Hutchinson. The Dynamic New Way to Create Successful Ideas Publisher: Classic Business Bookshelf (November 23, 2010) ISBN-10: 1608425614 ISBN-13: 978-1608425617
2. Rawlinson J. Geoffrey Creative Thinking and Brainstorming. Jaico Publishing House (April 30, 2005) ISBN-10: 8172243480 ISBN-13: 978-8172243487

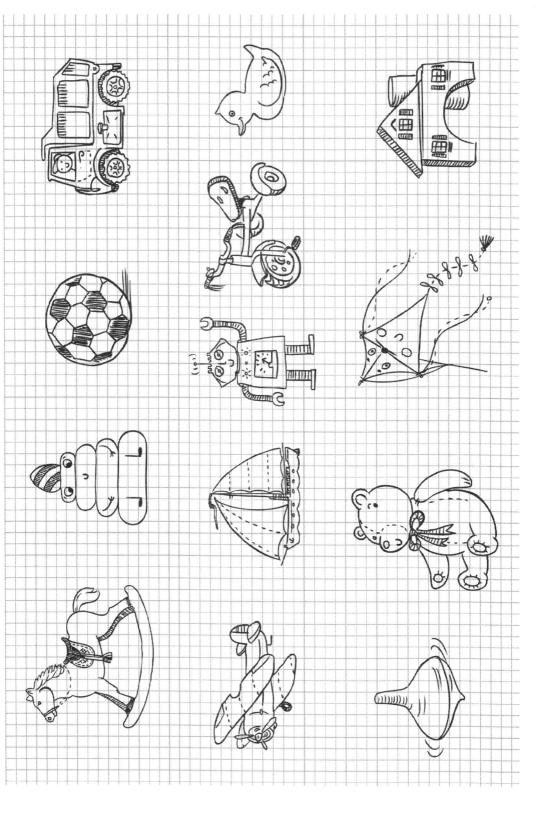

10 x 10 sketch method

WHAT IS IT?

This method is an approach to making early concept generation sketching more efficient in use of time than the method that stresses finished sketches early in the design process. It allows more time to explore ideas and so stresses the quality of thinking and the final solution. The 10 x 10 method involves creating ten rows with ten thumbnail sketches per row on each page.

WHY USE THIS METHOD?

1. It allows more exploration of alternative ideas in a shorter time
2. May lead to a final concept which is a better design than traditional approaches.
3. Prevents sketches from becoming jewelry in the mind of the designer and more important than the quality of the final design solution.

CHALLENGES

1. This method takes discipline

WHEN TO USE THIS METHOD

1. Explore Concepts

HOW TO USE THIS METHOD

1. Traditional design concept exploration involves a designer producing six to 12 alternative design concepts presented as attractive renderings
2. This method involves a designer making ten rows of ten simple fast cartoon like sketches per page.
3. Each sketch should be no larger than one inch by one inch.
4. The designer produces 5 to 20 pages of very fast sketches during first phase of concept exploration
5. Designs are reviewed and ranked by the design team following a discussion and presentation by the designer and a relatively small number are selected for iteration, recombination and further development.
6. At the next stage more finished and larger concept sketches are produced

RESOURCES

1. Paper
2. Fine line pens
3. Sharpie markers

Chapter 5
Generative workshops

generative prototyping

WHAT IS IT?

A method also called "Thinkering" where participants build simple prototypes from supplied materials to explore ideas.

WHO INVENTED IT?

Pioneered by Liz Sanders 2002 and Lego Johan Roos and Bart Victor 1990s.

WHY USE THIS METHOD?

1. Creative way to generate ideas involving users
2. Discovering user needs
3. Developing concepts with users
4. Designing prototypes with users

CHALLENGES

1. Demanding of participants:
2. Good moderation needed
1. Designers can become too attached to their prototypes and allow them to become jewelry that stands in the way of further refinement.

WHEN TO USE THIS METHOD

1. Know Context
2. Know User
3. Frame insights
4. Explore Concepts

HOW TO USE THIS METHOD

1. "In generative prototyping users are asked to together with designers built low-tech prototypes or products using a large set of materials during a workshop. For example, in creating ideas for a new playground, children were asked to built their favorite playground element using ice lolly sticks, foam balls, etc
2. The basic idea is that by building, you start thinking and new ideas are generated."

source: Geke Luken

RESOURCES

1. Toy construction kits such as lego
2. Pop sticks
3. String
4. Tape
5. Post-it-notes
6. Cardboard
7. Paper
8. Markers

REFERENCES

1. Statler, M., Roos, J., and B. Victor, 2009, 'Ain't Misbehavin': Taking Play Seriously in Organizations,' Journal of Change Management, 9(1): 87–107.

workshops: creative toolkits

WHAT IS IT?

Collections of modular objects that can be used for participatory modeling and prototyping to inform and inspire design teams. Often used in creative codesign workshops. It is a generative design method which facilitates creative play. The elements can be reused in a number of research sessions in different geographic locations.

WHO INVENTED IT?

Pioneered by Liz Sanders and Lego Johan Roos and Bart Victor 1990s.

WHY USE THIS METHOD?

Helps develop:
1. Problem solving
2. Change management
3. Strategic thinking
4. Decision making
5. Services, product and experience redesign
6. Can be fun
7. Identify opportunities
8. Re frame challenges
9. Leverages creative thinking of the team

WHEN TO USE THIS METHOD
1. Know Context
2. Know User
3. Frame insights
4. Explore Concepts

image: © Grandeduc | Dreamstime.com

HOW TO USE THIS METHOD
1. Form cross-disciplinary team 5 to 20 members. It's best to have teams of not more than 8
2. Identify design problem. Create agenda.
3. Start with a warming up exercise.
4. Write design problem in visible location such as white board.
5. Workshop participants first build individual prototypes exploring the problem.
6. Divide larger group into smaller work groups of 3 to 5 participants.
7. Ask each participant to develop between 1 and design solutions. Can use post-it notes or cards.
8. Through internal discussion each group should select their preferred group design solution.
9. The group builds a collective model incorporating the individual contributions.
10. Each group build a physical model of preferred solution and presents it to larger group.
11. Larger group selects their preferred design solutions by discussion and voting.
12. Capture process and ideas with video or photographs.
13. Debriefing and harvest of ideas.

REFERENCES

1. Statler, M., Roos, J., and B. Victor, 2009, 'Ain't Misbehavin': Taking Play Seriously in Organizations,' Journal of Change Management, 9(1): 87–107.

design charette

WHAT IS IT?

A design charette is a collaborative design workshop usually held over one day or several days. Charettes are a fast way of generating ideas while involving diverse stakeholders in your decision process. Charettes have many different structures and often involve multiple sessions. The group divides into smaller groups. The smaller groups present to the larger group.

WHO INVENTED IT?

The French word, "charrette" spelt with two r's means "cart" This use of the term is said to originate from the École des Beaux Arts in Paris during the 19th century, where a cart, collected final drawings while students finished their work.

WHY USE THIS METHOD?

1. Fast and inexpensive.
2. Increased probability of implementation.
3. Stakeholders can share information.
4. Promotes trust.

CHALLENGES

1. Managing workflow can be challenging.
2. Stakeholders may have conflicting visions.

WHEN TO USE THIS METHOD

1. Define intent
2. Know context and user
3. Frame insights
4. Explore concepts
5. Make Plans

RESOURCES

1. Large space
2. Tables
3. Chairs
4. White boards
5. Dry-erase markers
6. Camera
7. Post-it-notes

REFERENCES

1. Day, C. (2003). Consensus Design: Socially Inclusive Process. Oxford, UK, and Burlington, MA: Elsevier Science, Architectural Press.

1.5 day mini charette

HOW TO USE THIS METHOD

Day 1

1. Evening mixer night before event.
2. Breakfast 30 minutes.
3. Moderator introduces participants expectations and goals.
4. Overview of project 30 mins
5. Break 15 minutes
6. Individual presenters present information about aspects of project 1 hour
7. Lunch 1 hour
8. Further presentations related to aspects of project 1 hour
9. Question and answer session 15 minutes
10. Multi disciplinary breakout groups 2.5 hours
11. Group size preferred 4 to 8 participants.
12. Groups explore strategies and issues.
13. Groups present strategies and goals to larger group 30 minutes. Larger group brainstorms goals.
14. Site tour 1 hour - for urban or architectural projects.

Day 2

1. Breakfast 30 minutes
2. Review of Day 1, 30 minutes.
3. Breakout groups explore concept solutions as sketches 2.5 hours.
4. Groups present to larger group 30 minutes.
5. Larger group brainstorms next steps 30 minutes
6. Lunch 1 hour

RESOURCES

1. Large space
2. Tables
3. Chairs
4. White boards
5. Dry-erase markers
6. Camera
7. Post-it-notes

2.0 day design charette

HOW TO USE THIS METHOD
Day 1
1. Evening mixer night before event.
2. Breakfast 30 minutes.
3. Moderator introduces participants expectations and goals.
4. Overview of project 30 mins
5. Break 15 minutes
6. Individual presenters present information about aspects of project 1 hour
7. Lunch 1 hour
8. Further presentations related to aspects of project 1 hour
9. Question and answer session 15 minutes
10. Multi disciplinary breakout groups 2.5 hours
11. Group size preferred 4 to 8 participants.
12. Groups explore strategies and issues.
13. Groups present strategies and goals to larger group 30 minutes. Larger group brainstorms goals.
14. Site tour 1 hour - for urban or architectural projects.

Day 2
1. Breakfast 30 minutes
2. Review of Day 1, 30 minutes.
3. Breakout groups explore concept solutions as sketches 2.5 hours.
4. Groups present to larger group 30 minutes.
5. Lunch 1 hour
6. Breakout groups refine concept solutions as sketches 2.5 hours.
7. Groups present to larger group 30 minutes.
8. Wrap up and next steps 30 minutes

RESOURCES
1. Large space
2. Tables
3. Chairs
4. White boards
5. Dry-erase markers
6. Camera
7. Post-it-notes

4.0 day architectural charette

HOW TO USE THIS METHOD
1. Define problem
2. Public meeting Vision
3. Brief group
4. Alternative concepts generated
5. Small groups work
6. Small groups present.
7. Whole group discussion
8. Public meeting input
9. Preferred concepts developed
10. Small groups work
11. Small groups present.
12. Whole group discussion
13. Open house review
14. Small groups work
15. Small groups present.
16. Whole group discussion
17. Further plan development.
18. Public meeting confirmation of final design.

RESOURCES
1. Large space
2. Tables
3. Chairs
4. White boards
5. Dry-erase markers
6. Camera
7. Post-it-notes

635 method design charette

HOW TO USE THIS METHOD

1. Choose a problem to focus on.
2. Select moderator.
3. Select and invite participants.
4. Team size of 4 to 20 participants preferred representing users, managers, design and diverse group of stakeholders.
5. Break down teams into groups of 3 participants.
6. Each group of 3 should sit at a separate table.
7. Brief participants in advance by e-mail.
8. Allow one hour per problem
9. Use creative space such as a room with a large table and whiteboard.
10. Brief participants allow 15 minutes to one hour for individual concept exploration.
11. Can use egg timer to time sessions.
12. Give each participant a goal such as 5 concepts.
13. At end of concept exploration time group selects the best 3 concepts from the session and two participants move to another table. One participant stays at table.
14. The session is repeated each group combines the best ideas from two tables.
15. Repeat this process five times.
16. At the end of these concept exploration session pin all the drawings on a wall and group by affinities.
17. Moderator and group can evaluate the concepts using a list of heuristics.
18. Dot vote each category to determine best ideas to carry forward.
19. Do another round of sketching focusing of 3 best ideas.
20. Record session with digital images.
21. Smaller group can take preferred ideas and develop them after the session.

RESOURCES

1. Large space
2. Tables
3. Chairs
4. White boards
5. Dry-erase markers
6. Camera
7. Post-it-notes

0.5 day product design charette

HOW TO USE THIS METHOD

1. Choose a problem to focus on.
2. Select moderator.
3. Select and invite participants.
4. Team size of 4 to 20 participants preferred representing users, managers, design and diverse group of stakeholders.
5. Break down teams over 8 into smaller groups of 4 or 5 participants.
6. Brief participants in advance by e-mail.
7. Allow one hour per problem
8. Use creative space such as a room with a large table and whiteboard.
9. Brief participants allow 15 minutes to one hour for individual concept exploration.
10. Give participants a goal such as 5 concepts.
11. Output can be sketches or simple models using materials such as cardboard or toy construction kits.
12. Each individual presents their concepts to the group.
13. In larger groups each group of 4 can select 3 favored ideas in smaller group to present to larger group. Each smaller group selects a presenter.
14. Moderator and group can evaluate the concepts using a list of heuristics.
15. Put all the sketches or post it notes on a wall.
16. Group concepts into categories of related ideas.
17. Dot vote each category to determine best ideas to carry forward.
18. Do another round of sketching focusing of 3 best ideas.
19. Iterate this process as many times as necessary.
20. Record session with digital images.
21. Smaller group can take preferred ideas and develop them after the session.

RESOURCES

1. Large space
2. Tables
3. Chairs
4. White boards
5. Dry-erase markers
6. Camera
7. Post-it-notes
8. Materials such as cardboard, children's construction kits

0.5 day ux charette

HOW TO USE THIS METHOD

1. Choose a problem to focus on.
2. Select moderator.
3. Select and invite participants.
4. Team size of 4 to 20 participants preferred representing users, managers, design and diverse group of stakeholders.
5. Break down teams over 8 into smaller groups of 4 or 5 participants.
6. Brief participants in advance by email.
7. Allow one hour per problem
8. Use creative space such as a room with a large table and whiteboard.
9. Brief participants allow 15 minutes to one hour for individual concept exploration.
10. Give participants a goal such as 5 concepts.
11. Output can be wireframes or storyboards.
12. Each individual presents their concepts to the group.
13. Moderator and group can evaluate the concepts using a list of heuristics.
14. Put all the sketches or post it notes on a wall.
15. Group concepts into categories of related ideas.
16. Dot vote each category to determine best ideas to carry forward.
17. Do another round of sketching focusing of 3 best ideas.
18. Iterate this process as many times as necessary.
19. Record session with digital images.
20. Smaller group can take preferred ideas and develop them after the session.

RESOURCES

1. Large space
2. Tables
3. Chairs
4. White boards
5. Dry-erase markers
6. Camera
7. Post-it-notes

index

index

index

other titles in the
design methods series

Design Methods 1
200 ways to apply design thinking

Author: Robert A Curedale
Published by:
Design Community College Inc.
PO Box 1153
Topanga CA 90290 USA

Edition 1 November 2013

ISBN-10: 0988236206
ISBN-13: 978-0-9882362-0-2

Design Methods 2
200 ways to apply design thinking

Author: Robert A Curedale
Published by:
Design Community College Inc.
PO Box 1153
Topanga CA 90290 USA

Edition 1 January 2013

ISBN-10: 0988236214
ISBN-13: 978-0-9882362-1-9

Structured Workshops

The author presents workshops online and in person in global locations for executives, engineers, designers, technology professionals and anyone interested in learning and applying these proven innovation methods. For information contact: info@curedale.com

about the author

Rob Curedale was born in Australia and worked as a designer, director and educator in leading design offices in London, Sydney, Switzerland, Portugal, Los Angeles, Silicon Valley, Detroit, and China. He designed and managed over 1,000 products and experiences as a consultant and in-house design leader for the world's most respected brands. Rob has three decades experience in every aspect of product development, leading design teams to achieve transformational improvements in operating and financial results. He has extensive experience in forging strategic growth, competitive advantage, and a background in expanding business into emerging markets through user advocacy and extensive cross cultural expertise. Rob's designs can be found in millions of homes and workplaces around the world.

Rob works currently as a Adjunct Professor at Art Center College of Design in Pasadena and consults to organizations in the United States and internationally and presents workshops related to design. He has taught as a member of staff and presented lectures and workshops at many respected design schools and universities throughout the world including Yale, Pepperdine University, Art Center Pasadena, Loyola University, Cranbrook, Pratt, Art Center Europe; a faculty member at SCA and UTS Sydney; as Chair of Product Design and Furniture Design at the College for Creative Studies in Detroit, then the largest product design school in North America, Art Institute Hollywood, Cal State San Jose, Escola De Artes e Design in Oporto Portugal, Instituto De Artes Visuals, Design e Marketing, Lisbon, Southern Yangtze University, Jiao Tong University in Shanghai and Nanjing Arts Institute in China.

Rob's design practice experience includes projects for HP, Philips, GEC, Nokia, Sun, Apple, Canon, Motorola, Nissan, Audi VW, Disney, RTKL, Governments of the UAE,UK, Australia, Steelcase, Hon, Castelli, Hamilton Medical, Zyliss, Belkin, Gensler, Haworth, Honeywell, NEC, Hoover, Packard Bell, Dell, Black & Decker, Coleman and Harmon Kardon. Categories including furniture, healthcare, consumer electronics, sporting, homewares, military, exhibits, packaging. His products and experiences can be found in millions of homes and businesses throughout the world.

Rob established and manages the largest network of designers and architects in the world with more than 300,000 professional members working in every field of design.